Bittersweet
Lessons

Written by Nikki Nichole

D1637473

Bittersweet Lessons

This book is dedicated to the women of the world who are working hard while struggling to keep it all together. That woman who is feeling stuck or like your life is falling apart. To those who are in relationships that have gone sour but just do not know how to leave or aren't sure if they should. To them, who struggle with loving themselves enough or can't figure out how to shake their insecurities or low self-esteem. To the women who smile day in and day out but are secretly crying on the inside. This book is for you because I was you. I hope my story is able to help you see that it's never too late to change your story and have the life you want. Everything that you need to do it is already inside of you.

Bittersweet Lessons

Contents

Dear God..

Heavenly Father, I come first saying thank you. Thank you for your love, thank you for your grace, and thank you for your provision. You have never forsaken me even when I neglected to put you first in my life. You have extended your grace and mercy to me continuously, and I can never thank you enough. I come humbly asking you, Lord, to bless every reader of this book. I want to thank you for them, Lord, and I pray that they each receive something that they will benefit from in the reading. I pray that each person who reads this comes away feeling better and more empowered than when they went in. I pray that each person can tap into their inner strength and find the courage to do whatever is needed to gain peace, clarity, and happiness. Pour out a special blessing into each of their lives and give them an unwavering joy. Thank you for everything you have done in my life, everything you continue to do. I am nothing without you and your power in my life. I love you, and I trust you to get this book into the hands that need it most. In Jesus' name, Amen.

Bittersweet Lessons

Prologue

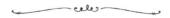

H ave you ever asked yourself how did I get here? Well, that is the question that I found myself mulling over after the demise of my fourteen-year marriage. There were so many thoughts, so many feelings, and so many questions. But, once I looked deeper, I saw that there were also so many lessons. Bittersweet Lessons.

After reflecting on all of my previous failed relationships, I realized that there were a lot of mistakes made, and many red flags missed. There were a lot of things that I wished someone would have shared with me or helped me with along the way. Something that could have possibly saved me from many of the bad or toxic relationships I endured. Although there was no one in my life to give me that very much needed advice, I understand that God makes no mistakes. Everything that I went through, I grew through, which brings us to this personal memoir. God showed me that my life is a testimony that is meant to be shared so that it can bless and help others.

I understand that the struggles I experienced were not meant to hurt me but to make me stronger and to help somebody else. There wasn't anyone around for me to seek advice from, so I knew in my heart that I had a responsibility to become that person. I saw a meme that said, "Be the person that you needed when you were younger," and that sums it up perfectly. I'm praying that the things I learned can hopefully help another sister who needs that advice, that boost, or simply... that reminder.

Inside this book, you will read about the entertaining and dramatic experiences in love that I've experienced. Stories that I know many can relate to and situations that are seemingly straight from a lifetime movie filled with young love, a teenage pregnancy, mental illness, abuse, kidnapping, and more! More importantly, you will also hear about the many life lessons in love and relationships that can only come from the wisdom gained from doing things the wrong way.

So, Sis, I hope you're ready for an unbelievable ride of highs and lows. You'll experience my journey through hard truths, questionable choices, and, ultimately, a transitioning through deep revelations, wisdom, and growth. A journey of Bittersweet Lessons that lead towards a new perspective on how to not just simply "love yourself" but to love yourself enough. These lessons are what empowered me into taking back my life and demanding a change. When you finally realize and learn to love yourself enough, you realize that the sky isn't even the limit! I have since become a successful entrepreneur, author, speaker, and women's empowerment specialist. My goal with this book is to help the women in the position that I was in to feel that empowerment to love themselves enough to leave any situation that doesn't serve them.

P.S. Please feel free to take a listen to the song titles attached to each mini chapter. My life's moments of highs and lows, have ultimately lead to a pretty dope soundtrack!! ♪

Part 1

My Life, My Story

Bittersweet Lessons

Chapter 1

In The Beginning

Little Girl Nikki
"Back In The Day" – Ahmad

Okay, so where do I begin? I guess I'll start at the beginning. When young little Nikki was a wee little girl. Little Nikki Nichole always had a dream of being married! She fantasized about it since playing the game "Life" as a little girl. There was just something about being a wife, a mother that equated to living the dream life, you know, just like her Barbie dolls did. Since I was about seven years old, I knew that I wanted to be a wife & mom, and I wanted to live that happily ever after life. You see, I grew up in poverty, the fourth and youngest girl to my single mom, who was divorced. My entire childhood and into adulthood, I never saw my mom work, nor in a relationship, so my young, naive mind led me to believe that if only she had a husband, we'd be more like the Huxtables on TV. I saw my mom struggle to make ends meet, and in my mind, I always knew that I had to make sure to do better when it was my turn. I wanted to make sure my kids had everything I saw the kids have on tv. In my little mind, that meant I needed a nice job, a husband, a house, two cars, kids, and a dog (go figure). Of course, the white picket fence was a part of the vision, but that fence part was negotiable... I'd be ok with any fence or no fence at all. I could definitely ixnay on the fence if all other areas were covered. My husband would be tall & handsome with a job; those were the only requirements in my seven-year-old mind. I would have 2-3 kids, two boys, and a girl. Lastly, we would own two cars and a huge house!! What I didn't know then in my little bit of time on earth is that all of that is very much attainable, but all of that is also very much a façade for true happiness.

I can recall growing up in my early days, always feeling like I wasn't good enough. I would get told I was pretty but never felt pretty enough. I felt like that was all some people would see that I was pretty, but they never really saw the real me, which a lot of the time was not very happy inside. I think my feelings of not being good enough came from my family not having money, constantly struggling with bills, and not having my father in the picture. My mom is one of the sweetest, kindest people you will ever meet, and she did her best but she was suffering from an illness which caused her to be unable to work. I used to wish all the time that my mom would be able to work so that we could finally have money. I didn't know at that time why she didn't, so it sometimes would make me angry. I looked around, and all that I saw was that my friends and peers all had young working parents who had some money and provided for their children. My mom provided for us as best she could, we never went without but she was limited with the amount of resources she had.

I would see my friends and peers with the latest shoes or name brand clothes, and I'd sit wishing I had the same. One time my older sister gave me some hand me down clothes and a long jean "Guess" skirt was in the bag. I loveeeeeeed that skirt because it was like my first piece of name brand clothing. Anytime my sisters or anyone would take me anywhere, I'd always go put on my skirt to feel like I had name brand stuff. The skirt was too big for me and very loose, but I did not care; I would roll the waist part down to make it stay up. It is funny, thinking back about it now, but I was so seriously proud of that skirt back then.

I have another distinctive memory. Most people probably do not remember, but Payless used to have a brand of shoes called Prowings, and they were considered the lowest of the low, so nobody wanted to step foot in them. I, however, had no choice because that is all my mom could afford, and my dad wasn't really around and did not help out very much. So I am sure you can imagine the embarrassment of having to wear Prowings to school each day and being teased or talked about. I had thick skin and held my own for the most part. I wasn't the type to go home crying because I was being capped on, no, not at all. I always stood up for myself and made sure to dish it back out to those bullies. I can remember asking my older cousin to get me some shoes because he always dressed fresh and had money. He promised me he would, but each time I saw him, he had nothing for me. Finally, after I don't know how long, my older cousin came through, buying me some Nike Cortez shoes!! Fun Fact: Ironically, the name of the shoe is also his name. Let me just tell you that my little heart was so happy and grateful I didn't know what to do. I probably had never smiled so big in my life. I was elated to have those shoes!! I was so happy and excited because I felt like those shoes validated me just like the skirt. It was my first pair of name brand shoes.

I was so disappointed about not having much as a kid that I couldn't wait to have a chance to make my own money. As soon as I got fourteen-years-old, the legal age to work with a work permit, I signed up to work for the youth summer work program, a program for low-income teens to work during the summer. I remember getting my first job in an office in an apartment complex called KO. I was making $4.25 an hour, and I was so excited to finally have some cash in my pocket. Every summer, I signed up for the program and worked for my own money until I was able to get a real job.

Seemingly having one of my problems partially solved by working and making my own money, I could buy my own clothes and update my wardrobe before high school started. I was able to step my game up a little bit and wear clothes that I felt good about.

But, having a little bit of money did not fix some of my other problems, such as my relationship with my mostly absentee father.

My father was truly a rolling stone. He had kids of all ages, sizes, and in several different area codes. He had his first child in Minneapolis, Minnesota, at the age of 15 and continued to populate the world with more of his offspring - well into his 60s. To his credit, he always claimed all of his children. He was around for some of them, but there simply was no way for him to take care of all of them financially, emotionally, or otherwise. So although I knew who my father was and he would come by every so often and drop off a few dollars to my mom, he didn't raise me. He always made me feel special and loved when he did come around, but having that inconsistency in one of your most important relationships caused some feelings of insecurity and not being good enough. I always felt like the kids he lived with had it better than I did and that they were lucky to have both a mom and a dad in the home, but little did I know it wasn't all peaches and cream over there either.

It's funny because I remember as I grew into my teenage years, I started to understand that my life was dysfunctional. My mom did her best, and I appreciate her but it still was a dysfunctional environment. My dad lived in the same city as me, and I hardly saw him unless it was a special event such as a birthday party or graduation. My dad always made sure to tell me he loved me, and yes, I believed him. I appreciated him showing me that I was loved. I also appreciated the things he did show up for like my graduations and some birthday parties, but I still had a void there. I think that inside I kinda felt like that you may have to settle for a man's love in some way or fashion. I grew accustomed to settling for what I could get from my dad instead of understanding fully how I deserved more. Thinking back, I didn't hear the words "I love you" much from my mom either, but she most definitely showed it in action.

I bet you're wondering why I'm mentioning all of this when this book is supposed to be about my relationship lessons. Well, I do believe, after looking back, that I accepted some things within relationships and stayed in some of them too long because of some of my inner feelings, fears, and doubts deriving from my childhood. As I got older, I would learn quite a few lessons about love & relationships, and unfortunately, most times, they were lessons learned the hard way.

Bittersweet Lessons

Relationship Ground Zero
"Here We Go Again" – Portrait

I met my oldest son's father at a festival. I was fifteen years old, and he was sixteen. I remember attending the festival with my best friend Jenise and catching him staring at me from across the street. At this point in my life, I was considered a "square" because I didn't hang out like other kids in the neighborhood. I didn't hang out much because my mom was very strict and kept me sheltered. So I didn't know a lot of people, and a lot of people didn't know me. I saw him staring and could tell he was interested by the smirk on his face. I thought he was kinda cute, so I asked my bestie if she knew who he was. My best friend knew exactly who he was from the neighborhood and told me that he was cool. Eventually, he came over and introduced himself to me and asked to exchange phone numbers. I gave him my number and left the festival excited about the possibilities.

I was going to the 10th grade, and I was a virgin. By now, I had only had two boyfriends well, really one and a half, because the first one was more like a peer pressure thing. I was in 6th grade, and he was in 8th grade, and I was just excited that a boy wanted me to be his girlfriend, so I said yes. I didn't really like him nor want to do anything boyfriends and girlfriends do. That first boyfriend experience was a bit stressful for me because he would walk me home every day and wanted to tongue kiss. I was too young to know how to kiss. So, I was too scared to do it and would tell him no every single time. But he was persistent and wouldn't give up. One day, he got a whole crew of friends together, and they all joined us on the way to walk me home, and the goal of this gang of folks was to try and convince me that I should stop being scared and to just kiss him. I was soooo embarrassed and scared and felt so much pressure the whole walk home. When we got there, I had to decide if I would do it or "be a baby" as a few of them in the group referred to it as. I was no more than 12 years old and pressured into doing something I didn't feel comfortable doing. Even thinking back about that time now gives my stomach an uneasy feeling. I didn't want to do it, and so when we got to my stoop at my house, they all stood around in expectation, wondering if their plan and taunts had worked. He shooed them away so that he and I could be alone and then the moment of truth arrived, and I had to decide on what I was going to do. I decided at that moment that I was NOT going to kiss this damn boy! NO! I didn't care what the group thought, what he felt, or how it made me look like a baby. I am proud to say that in my earliest memories of being a young girl, I was always seemingly strong enough to stand up for myself and not do something that I really didn't want to do. The flipside of that is that if I really want to do something, I will, and not many people can change my mind.

So back to my first real relationship. I was at a place in my life now, where I was ready to experience more. I was tired of being sheltered, and I felt like I was ready to lose my virginity. I decided in my mind that he was worthy, and we developed a whirlwind of a relationship. Things happened pretty fast and very intensely. He introduced me to a totally different way of life. For one, he was one of the guys who hung out in the streets, so for the first time. I was hanging out too. He was so very sweet & loving to me and expressed his love to me quite early on and quite often. I, however, didn't know what love was or how it was supposed to feel or be. I had no examples around me growing up, so I was confused. I knew that I liked him a lot, but I couldn't determine if it was love or not. He sort of pressured me into "loving" him, and so at that point, our love affair began. When I say pressured me, I mean he kept asking me if I loved him because he felt that he loved me and wanted me to say it. After a while, I said it back, but I honestly didn't believe that I was in love. Thinking back on it now, we were teens, so I know for a fact that I wasn't in love. I was just in "like" or in "lust" and was very naïve.

We had many ups and downs, and back then, I wasn't very confident and vocal, although I was always very strong-willed, smart, and a deep thinker. I used to always struggle with feeling like I wasn't good enough. My clothes were not the latest, I didn't have the newest Jordan's, and my body was still developing so in teenage terms, which made you popular or fit in I didn't have. I didn't have money to do much or go anywhere, so it was pretty cool being with my boyfriend because he used to make me feel like I was good enough, plus he had money and was very generous. He had a very kind and selfless spirit about him. His core was good, and he always would say he had a good heart, which he really did. I remember he came upon a lot of money from doing something illegal, and he took me shopping at Stonestown mall, a mall right outside of San Francisco. I don't think I'd ever been there before that time, so I was so happy and excited. He had me cut school so that we could spend the day together. I would often cut school or classes now and then to spend time with him because I still wasn't given much freedom from my mom at this age, so I had to find creative ways to sneak and see him.

After a while, I felt like our relationship wasn't what I wanted any longer. I felt like he was a bad influence, and I actually wanted to be with someone who went to school with me. So I broke it off with him. I left that relationship to begin another with a high school sweetheart. I was a cheerleader/song-girl, and my boyfriend was on the football team, so it kind of fit the narrative of the perfect boyfriend/girlfriend situation you see on TV, such as saved by the bell.

When I broke up with my first, I broke his heart, and I didn't even realize how much. He had never been in love before, and neither had I. I still wasn't even sure if it was ever loved, I was feeling. But he seemed to be very confident. He didn't take the breakup well at all. He wouldn't leave me alone and wanted us to get back together. I can remember feeling bad, but I had made my decision. He found out about my new relationship and was not very happy. He made sure both of us knew of his displeasure with our relationship. After a while, he stopped pursuing me and left me alone.

Well, that new relationship didn't last long at all because I didn't feel that love vibe feeling from him like I got from my ex. He and I got along well, but he lived so far away, and I was restricted so much that we really couldn't carry on a real relationship. I really liked him a lot, but it just wasn't going to work. So I broke it off and did something that I later regretted, I went back to my ex. At the time, I didn't know what I was doing navigating through life, and I, unfortunately, didn't have anyone around giving me advice or advising me on life decisions. My older sisters are all 9+ years older than me, so they were all off living their own lives, and my mother never really felt comfortable talking to me about the birds & the bees or him, her and she's. Most of the advice I got from my friends who were around the same age as me, so I'm sure you can imagine just how well that went. We all were the blind leading the blind.

When I got back together with my first guy, things went well for a long while. Up until he turned around seventeen. You see, he began hanging out with older guys in the neighborhood, "His big homies" who had extremely negative ways of thinking about women. They believed that women were lesser than and not equals. Women were supposed to listen to their man and worship the ground he walked on. Well, for a girl like me who came from a household of little affection and had limited ideas around what relationships should be (outside of what I saw on TV and what my Barbie and Ken dolls did), I didn't have that instinct in me. What little bit I did know about relationships was enough to know that their chauvinist mindset was straight DUMB as hell. But unfortunately, he was still very impressionable in his mind and maturity, so he began to absorb the "game" they were giving him. For those who don't know, "game" is what you call advice in the hood. So basically, they gave him a bunch of "hood advice." This led to our relationship slowly breaking down. All of a sudden, he felt like I didn't adore him enough, I didn't show him enough love or affection, I didn't treat him like other girls treated their man, I didn't cater to him, I wasn't loud and boastful about our love, and I didn't listen. His big homies also instilled in him that all girls were cheaters **insert eye roll**, so this created a paranoia within him that, from that point on, just continued to fester and grow. He began accusing me of cheating on him, and after a while, he had convinced himself it was true. I'd never once cheated on him and was thoroughly confused by his change in behavior. He would go from being attentive & caring to mean and aggressive, all within the same conversation. It got really bad and unpredictable. I didn't know it then, but he was suffering from something deeper than just immaturity and ignorant thinking.

Introducing Abuse
"Love is Blind" – Eve

More time passed, and after a while, he became increasingly abusive, both verbally and physically, and I was terrified of him. His behavior changed so dramatically during this timeframe that I knew there had to be something deeper wrong. He began to lose touch with reality, and it was getting really bad. I can remember when he told me about hearing voices in his head that were telling him things. Or when he began realizing that the street signs had hidden messages. It was unfortunate and terrifying to watch him get more and more paranoid and out of control. He would hear things that were not there and see things that were not happening. He would often talk to himself and believed he was being watched. I was very concerned because he wasn't like this all the time, and when he was back to normal, he had no memory of his weird actions. One day I looked up the symptoms of his behaviors, and I realized that I was right. There was something more going on. According to what I'd read, he was paranoid schizophrenic. He would be completely normal and loving & kind one moment, but then he'd switch up out of nowhere and threaten and berate me. He would accuse me of looking at other men or flirting with other men, which was completely crazy. I wasn't even that type of girl. He wasn't even aware of his bizarre behavior and wouldn't believe anyone when we tried to tell him how he needed help.

I was completely terrified of him, but I kept it all inside. I was too embarrassed to share with anyone all of the things happening to me. Since he never really forgave me for breaking up with him that first time, he would often bring it up and use it as a reason to mistreat me. He would talk about it to make me feel like I made a huge mistake by leaving him the first time. I already felt that way, but I began to believe it even more now because he never acted crazy like this when we were together the first time. So I began to believe that it might've been my fault in some ways. I would try my best to keep things together and keep him from flipping out on me, sometimes it worked, and other times it didn't matter what I did or said, or how calm and docile I remained, he was going to go off. I knew that I probably needed to end the relationship, but I felt that he still could change. I also suspected that the way he was acting, he would never just let me leave. There was so much inner turmoil that I felt inside, knowing I was miserable but making sure that I didn't show it. So nobody else really knew.

After a while, I saw an expiration date for the abusive relationship I was in, but I voluntarily stayed in denial about it. I knew that his unpredictable behavior and propensity for paranoia and abuse would eventually push me away permanently. By now, he was so hot and cold that I couldn't keep up. He wasn't just physically abusive. He would also abuse me verbally & emotionally. He'd talk about me so badly that I'd be in tears contemplating just how true those accusations were. He'd always say that I was not like other girls, I wasn't good for nothing, I was stupid, I didn't know how to treat a man, I would never keep a man, I was worthless, etc. One thing about the physical abuse was that he always made sure to only hit or punch me in the arms or legs, or he'd push or choke me in ways so that it wouldn't mess up my face and so there would be nothing evident on the outside. He never wanted to mess up my face because he wanted me to stay pretty. So he made sure to keep the outside intact while constantly tearing me apart on the inside. My self-esteem was shredded to pieces during this time of my life. At an age where you are learning who you are and learning about how to love and value yourself, I was being led down a path of devalued self-worth. I wanted out, but I didn't know-how. I was too scared to say anything and also too afraid to leave.

I didn't have a lot of people in my life helping me and advising me through life's decisions as a teen. I mostly used common sense and friends' advice. One thing that I was afraid of was getting pregnant. It almost seemed like he was actively trying to get me pregnant because he started refusing to use protection. He also would force sex, whether I wanted to do it or not. The worst was an early evening when he was having an "episode" and as we walked through the neighborhood, we took a shortcut through a park, and it was then that he decided he wanted to have sex. I refused to strip down and have sex right there in the park. He grew increasingly upset at me, saying that I wasn't giving him what he needed, and he then started acting crazy and forcibly threw me down on the ground. I remember laying in the dirt/grass looking up at the sky, and it was a dark purple-ish color, not quite blue but also not quite black yet. I could see the moon shining, and it was so very quiet. There was a slight wind blowing on my face, and he was on top of me with a look on his face that can only be described as possessed. He wasn't taking no for an answer this time, and he proceeded to have sex with me while I laid there paralyzed crying. I remember looking up and hating my life at that moment.

Without being on any birth control and having very little control over things, I became pregnant at 17 1/2yrs old. I was planning to get an abortion as soon as I found out because I had no plans of having a kid so soon. I was so devastated and scared at first because I knew that this news would disappoint a lot of people. This was not the life I'd planned on having. I didn't want to fall into any of the negative stereotypes out there for black girls from the ghetto, and I had no plans to become a "baby mother" or even a single mother. I knew that I was too smart & capable of letting myself become just another stereotypical teen mom. I remember sitting there with a huge knot in my stomach because I didn't know what I would do with a kid. I was still a kid myself, plus I'd seen my mom struggle financially all my life, and since I knew that we both had no real money, I knew this meant I was creating the same life for my child.

He was strongly against me getting an abortion and promised he would be better, treat me better, and that we would get married and be a happy family. He was ecstatic about the baby and assured me that with a baby on the way, he was a better man. This baby had changed him for the better is what he said, and I believed him for the most part. I am also thinking that because I always dreamed of being married. It was easier to choose to believe him. Plus, I kept thinking back to how good things used to be when we first got together, and I kept hoping that someday we would make our way back to that happy place.

So I stayed with him, and after discussing with family & friends, I decided to also keep the baby. I have to say that I was close to getting an abortion, though. So close that I was actually at the appointment, legs up in stirrups waiting for the Dr to come in. But fifteen minutes before that moment, I was on the phone with my oldest sister. At the end of that conversation, she said to me, "You know you really don't have to do this if you don't want to. You have support and will be okay." Fast forward to being in the room thinking back on that conversation, looking over at the sonogram they were doing. I could have sworn I saw a baby boy with a diaper on in that image. That was my baby in there. That was my flesh and blood. At that moment, I decided that I no longer wanted to do the abortion, so I let the nurse know to cancel the procedure. One of my best friends was pregnant as well, and so I didn't feel entirely isolated in going through this experience so young, alone.

My friends rallied around me and provided me lots of mental & emotional support, but they also really had no idea how much turmoil I was truly in.

During my pregnancy, it was more of the same. He was nice & loving one minute and completely crazy the next. He really did try to be decent at first. The first few months after finding out, he was very loving and supportive and stayed in good spirits. But that didn't last long, as he couldn't quite control his episodes or paranoia. Since I got pregnant while still in high school, I had to go to prom pregnant. Luckily, I wasn't very far along, about 4 ½ months or so, so I could hide it in the dress I chose. Prom night for me was very traumatizing. He was my date for prom, and he dressed up nicely. We looked great together, and he was pretty amazing in preparing to make sure things went well. He arranged for our transportation, got us a room, and planned on a nice dinner after the prom was over. I loved my prom dress, a fitted, sparkling silver spaghetti strap pencil dress with a completely sheer mesh black covering.

I felt so pretty and lucky to be able to go to prom with my boyfriend of two years, who I knew wanted to marry me and start a family with me. It's crazy what we believe we want and need while we are still young. Here I was after just turning eighteen years old, thinking that I had my life figured out. Well, things did not go according to plan. Once we arrived at the prom, he became very upset with me for speaking to or chit-chatting with my friends. He especially got angry if I said hi or anything to any of my guy friends. He was also mad because he didn't know anybody there (since he didn't attend that school) and that I seemed to be more interested in talking to other people than to him. But the reality was, I was only being cordial and speaking to people who I had genuine friendships with. He had such a bad attitude that I felt like I was walking on eggshells, afraid of doing or saying the wrong thing. I didn't know if his temper would get the best of him, and I didn't want to be embarrassed, so I tried to play it as cool as possible. After a little while, I just sat there at a table with him damn near the entire time, without dancing or having any fun with him or my friends. He was mad, so he wouldn't even speak to me, so we sat there watching everybody else. I was miserable and genuinely wanted to cry. It was written all over my face because a couple of people even came up to me and asked me if I was okay. I wasn't, but of course, I lied and said that I was fine. After prom was over, I eventually ended up in tears because he kept on yelling at me and accusing me of craziness. I only wanted to have a good night, and yet here we were with him throwing insults at me left and right, making me feel like I was trash. So basically, prom for me was a horrible experience.

I didn't think that things could get any worse. He was so controlling and temperamental that I had no idea what the right things were to say. It was always changing, and he would always find something wrong with whatever I did. Things, however, did get a lot worse. While I was six months pregnant, one of the worst experiences of my life happened. The abuse amplified to the most severe level.

That day, we had a nice time together hanging out, and it was a beautiful day. We were back at his house in his room, just hanging out. It had been some time since the last time he flipped out on me, so I was feeling happy and hopeful. I remember thinking that this was a good day and that there was possibly a chance we were making our way back to that happy place. That feeling didn't last very long. Out of nowhere, he suddenly became paranoid and convinced himself that I was cheating on him. He was now upset because he said he just knew I'd cheated and that the baby probably wasn't even his baby. He had absolutely no viable reason to think or believe this, but the voices in his mind told him I was, so he was convinced I was cheating. He and I got into a very heated argument, and I tried so hard to get him to see the truth, but he just couldn't. It was so disheartening to hear that he didn't trust me when I'd been nothing but loyal to him.

I'd stuck by his side throughout his downward spiral through these several months of unpredictable behaviors, always the one trying to help him get better and be better. He worked himself up into rage during this particular argument, and then he put his hands around my neck and choked me out. I remember his grip being so damn tight around my neck and me standing on my tiptoes, trying to gain footing. This moment was one of the absolute scariest moments of my life. He was not himself. He would not listen to reason, he would not calm down, and he would not stop no matter how hard I tried to claw his hands from me. As he choked me, I looked in his eyes, and I truly didn't recognize him. It was like he wasn't even there, not the person I knew and cared for. He was choking me, and he wasn't even there. I knew that he'd kill me if I didn't fight, and he wouldn't even probably remember it. I felt like I was slipping away and knew that it wouldn't be long before I passed out and possibly died.

Let's not forget that I was six months pregnant. I was struggling to breathe and felt my eyes watering. I didn't want to panic, but I also didn't want to die. More importantly, I didn't want my baby to die. He choked me for so long that I devised a plan to save my baby and myself in desperation. I decided to pretend to pass out so that he would stop choking me before I did pass out. So as a last-ditch effort, I stopped clawing and kicking at him, I stopped trying to fight him off of me, and I allowed my body to go limp and my eyes to close. My plan worked because he immediately let me go, and I allowed my body to drop to the ground, and as I hit the ground, I made sure to take a long deep breath without him seeing me. I wanted him to think that I was dead.

He instantly became regretful and began to cry and apologize. He kept asking himself, "What did I do?" "What did I do?" He started shaking me and begging me to wake up. I stayed completely still until I absolutely couldn't hold my breath anymore, and I finally had to let out a long breath. After letting out the long breath, I'd been holding. I played it off as best as possible and started coughing and acting like I was regaining consciousness. He was so scared and visibly shaken that he believed the entire stunt. He also was so apologetic that I knew then he was completely out of control. If you can flip a switch and aggressively attack the person you claim to love and then have so much remorse after, you are a danger to be around. I knew 100% that if I didn't get away, he would kill me and possibly our child.

A Life Of Torment
"Be Happy" - Mary J. Blige

My pregnancy continued to be horrible. I had very little relief from his constant abusive behavior. It was like he thrived on making me feel wrong about something. He'd always figure out more insults to use on me. He talked about me badly and always made me feel small and like I couldn't ever do anything right. He ended up getting arrested for a petty crime, and while he was in jail for that, I gave birth to our baby boy. My son's birth probably saved my life because my son became my hidden strength and my ultimate motivation. You see, I had never before experienced the real true rawest form of love until I laid eyes on my baby boy. Once my son was born, I knew I had to make some changes. His life was a priority for me. I now had to think of someone else's well-being over my own.

My son's father was released when our son was about six or seven months old, and despite the jailhouse letters full of promises of change, the various forms of abuse continued non-stop. He didn't care that I was the only one caring for and providing for our child. He didn't care that if I lost my job, our son would lack what he needed. He literally would sometimes refuse to let me leave his house even if it was for me to go to work. There were times that I had to call into my job with a made-up excuse for why I couldn't make it to work. He got me fired from my first real job by doing this. I was working for Popeye's, and although he knew I had to go to work, he started an argument with me and then refused to let me leave. I had one too many last-minute call-ins, so they fired me even though I was an excellent employee otherwise.

He continued to terrorize me month after month. He would be waiting outside for me to leave the house and then get in my face and talk smack or he would push me around or threaten me. I was terrified to leave the house sometimes because I didn't know if he'd be waiting. I was still suffering all of this in silence because I was too embarrassed to share it with anybody. I felt like he was right about being stupid because I had stupidly gotten myself into this horrible situation.

Once our son turned 10months old, his father did what I finally considered the last straw. After an argument about something he had made up in his head, He kidnapped our son from my house. I remember we were in front of my sister's house (whom I was living with). Our son was sitting in his playpen, playing with toys. I remember him getting super mad at me for reasons unknown. He kept his voice low because he didn't want to alarm my family, who were in the other room. He never wanted anyone to know that he was abusing me. Suddenly he jumps up and goes and grabs my son out of his playpen then storms out of the house.

I immediately hopped up and went to the phone on the wall in the kitchen and dialed 911. I had never once called the police on him, never once got the police involved or anyone else for that matter out of fear of what he'd do to me. I was so embarrassed about people finding out how stupid I was that I always kept things to myself. But in this instance, all bets were off!!! You snatched my son and took off, so I no longer cared what anyone thought. My only thoughts were surrounding me getting my son back. I didn't care what he felt about me calling the police. I didn't care about what my family would think who were in the next room. I also didn't care about the repercussions from him once he realized I finally told. I gathered every broken piece inside of me and used it as fuel for strength to finally speak up and say something! I dialed 911, and my sister and family were all looking at me trying to figure out what's going on. I proceeded to tell the operators that his unstable father kidnapped my son, and I needed help. My sister began questioning me immediately, and it was at that moment that the folks closest to me finally found out about some of the silent abuse I'd been going through.

He took our son & kept him from me for days. I had never gone one day without being with my son, so those were the most torturous days I'd ever experienced. I tried searching for them, but he wasn't at home or any other places I knew about. I had no idea where he and my son were, or if he was keeping my son safe. He had no food/formula for him, diapers, or clothing because he took him without his diaper bag. I also didn't know if he would do something to our son to hurt me, so I was beyond worried! My son was my life, and I was very serious about protecting my baby with my life, so it was killing me to not know where he was or if he was ok. I constantly prayed for God to protect my baby and bring him home. After two days, my best friend and I were outside when he rolled by on a bike. I was mortified to see him casually rolling around instead of somewhere taking care of our damn son. I asked him where our son was, and he just smirked at me and rolled away. I then went to the police station frantic for follow up and they told me that there was nothing they could do without a court order showing I had custody. I tried everything I could think of to get them to help me, I told them about him being unstable, about him owning a gun, about his threats and stalkerish behavior, but they did nothing. I was at the lowest point of my life, not knowing if my baby was safe or not.

After two days, which felt more like two weeks, he called me and told me that I could come and get the baby from him. He wouldn't give me an address. He told me to meet him at the corner near his house and told me to come alone. I wasn't sure if he would keep his word or do something to me, so I asked my brother in law to go with me. Everyone now knew about what he had been doing, so now I wasn't afraid to ask for the support I needed. My brother in law walked me to the destination he told me to meet him at, and as he saw us walking up, I could see the disappointment in his face of me not coming alone. I knew that he wanted me to go alone to control me and the situation in the way he wanted to. He probably didn't even plan to give my son back. He probably was planning to take me too. So as we walked up, he began strolling ahead of us without saying a word. He walked, and we trailed behind him, expecting him to take us to my baby. We ended up walking over to some apartments, which happened to be less than a mile away from where I lived with my sister. As soon as we went upstairs and inside of the apartment, I laid eyes on my baby. A guy in a wheelchair was holding him, and there were some other people around who went into a room when we came in. I immediately walked past everybody and went and grabbed my baby from the stranger's hands. He was naked with just a diaper and onesie t-shirt on, and he had drool running down his mouth and chest, but as soon as he saw me, his signature smile on his face lit up, and my heart exploded with relief, love, and joy. I was so grateful to God that my baby was safe. I can't even explain what my heart felt like. I was truly overjoyed. Leaving with my son, I knew that this relationship was officially OVER over. For the first time, that inner voice inside of me wasn't little anymore. It became an inner scream, yelling out to me: "Leave Him!" I knew I had to listen!

Helpless
"Get Away" - Bobby Brown

After the kidnapping of our son, I was done! I'd finally reached my breaking point. I finally built up enough strength and courage to do whatever it took to get away. I refused to give any more energy towards this toxic relationship. Endangering our son was the final straw. Like I said earlier, when it came to my son, I had strength and determination in ways that I can't even explain. So I cut off all communication with him. After realizing that this time was different and I was indeed done for good, he spiraled out of control. He refused to accept the fact that I was done, and there was nothing he could do or say to change my mind. I was still very much afraid of him and afraid of what he might do, but I was more afraid of exposing myself and my son to any more trauma. He began to completely terrorize me by calling me back to back over 100 times a day, following me, stalking me, threatening me. This was not the same guy with the kind heart id met almost four years ago. This was a totally different person he had morphed into.

I had no car, so I had to walk to the public bus to work each day. This one time, he caught me while I was on my way to work, and he grabbed me and forced me to go with him against my will. He had a knife, and I already knew he owned a gun, so I avoided setting him off to do something violent. He had nowhere for us to go, so we just walked throughout the neighborhood while he talked down to me, called me names, and kept kicking me. It was so embarrassing because people were walking by, some gawking and others seemingly concerned. The people staring didn't seem to bother or embarrass him at all because he kept abusing me.

Lots of people had looks of concern, but nobody said or did anything. Cars were driving by, and I could see people looking, but nobody stopped. My heart was beating so fast because I didn't know if today would be the day that he would take my life. As he continued to hit & punch me while we walked down the street, all I could do is cry. I remember feeling helpless and thinking that I was stuck in this life/situation, and I couldn't do anything about it. I knew without a shadow of a doubt that this man was going to end up killing me. I mean, he had almost done it already. But I couldn't let that happen, I had a son out there that needed me, and I was determined to be around for him. After a while, he pulled out a black and mild cigar, lit it, and then started putting it close to my face threatening to burn my face. He kept taunting me with it, and I kept moving my face each time. He then grabbed my left hand and smashed the burning cigar into the middle of my hand. I screamed out in pain and snatched my hand away. He told me to be quiet, or he would do more, so I cried silently.

Somehow I always hoped that my tears and agony would jolt some sort of remembrance inside of him. I always secretly wished that he'd see how much he was hurting me and that the love he had inside would snap him out of his trance. I remember that day crying so hard but trying to be silent, and as I looked at him, I realized my tears would never be enough to stop him from hurting me.

A little while later, a police officer walked up to us and asked me if I was okay. I am assuming that someone had called since we were out on the public streets. But I was too afraid to say that I was in trouble to the officer in front of him, so I told the officer that I was fine, but I kept purposefully wiping my eyes with my left hand so he'd notice my burn. He didn't see it, or he didn't care, and since I said I was fine, he left. I remember thinking that here my stupid butt was making another stupid decision and feeling like shit. But I was just so scared of him and of what he might do. I knew that he was very likely going to kill me if I didn't get away from him, but I didn't want him to know or see me going against him out of fear he'd get to me first before the cops could, and he would hurt me. So I wanted the help, but I didn't want to do anything to make the stalking, threats, and abuse even worse. He eventually let me go home after several hours of me pleading with him that I needed to get home to get more baby formula for our son. It was late and dark outside when he finally let me leave, so I didn't feel comfortable walking to the store to get the formula. I felt like such an awful mother, but I didn't want him to come out of the cuts again and attack me.

During this time, I was still very much determined to provide for my son and not give him a life of struggle like I had. I started an internship at UCSF hospital and worked hard. They then added me as a permanent employee, and I began making a decent salary. I finally got a car, which helped me feel a little better, but I still had to walk to my car, hoping and praying that he wouldn't pop out on me. I was always scared to death and would try to park as close to my front door as possible and then pretty much run to and from my car. He seemed to always be somewhere watching because he would call and tell me how he'd seen me and describe what I had on and everything I did. This was before we had the luxury of being able to block people's calls. He had increasingly gotten worse in his episodes where he lost touch with reality. He sometimes would make sense, and sometimes would not. He did, however, make it clear that no matter where I went, he was always going to know. He also made it clear that if he couldn't have me, then that meant nobody would. This was far before there was a whole network (LMN) dedicated to Lifetime movies, and yet and still, I'd seen enough of those movies on the regular lifetime channel to know that I was right to feel like my life was in danger. I didn't know what to do. I was terrified.

Church
"More On me" - Kirk Franklin

A friend of mine invited me to her church, and I decided to go, and I ended up re-accepting God into my life. I had attended her church a few times before while we were in high school, but outside of that, I hadn't been to church since I was a little girl. I always felt like God and the church were a safe haven, and I desperately needed safety. I was in a place in life where I knew that the only person who could help me was God, and so I began to attend church with her regularly. My life was still being terrorized, but I remember having some semblance of peace & happiness inside knowing and trusting that God had his hand on my life. I enjoyed bringing my son to church with me, as well. I remember this one day, specifically when things with my ex became so overwhelming that I recall going up to the altar and crying like a baby. My ex-relationship was the cause of so much distress and turmoil in my life. I was absolutely terrified of him since his episodes were to a point where they were more on than off, meaning he was out of his mind at least 85% of the time and only in touch with reality around 15%. I prayed harder than I'd ever prayed before, asking God to please save me from this relationship. I asked God to please save me and to help him. I needed God to fix this situation, and I left my entire heart on that altar. When I got up and went back to my seat, I was filled with sudden calmness and an unexplainable confirmation that everything would be alright. I didn't know how, but I knew that God had my back and would help me out of this situation.

A few days later, I came outside one day to see that he had scratched my new car up. The car had deep, angry scratches on the side. How I knew for a fact that it was him was the fact that he'd scratched his entire nickname into my driver's side door except for the last two letters. It was as if someone stopped him before he was able to finish. I was so hurt. This was the very first car that I'd purchased for myself from the dealership. It was a Mitsubishi Mirage and was my favorite color, red. I loved my car and loved being able to provide transportation for my son and me. When I saw what he'd done to my car, I was livid. I walked around, feeling miserable as hell and couldn't do a thing about it. I was smiling on the outside in front of my friends and family but crying like a baby inside.

I knew God was going to work it out. I just wasn't sure how or when.

I filed a police report on what he did to my car, and while there, I finally spilled the beans on everything else he had been doing. I told them about every instance of abuse from A to Z. After leaving the police department and making the report, I felt guilty. I knew that I was doing the right thing, but I couldn't shake the feeling that I'd just escalated things to another level. The police officers advised me to get a restraining order, and I began to consider it. I wanted to get it, but I knew that a piece of paper could not protect me from someone unstable and intent on hurting me. I didn't want to get the restraining order, and it becomes the cause for him to lose all control and decide to kill our child or me. I had so much turmoil inside and nowhere to turn for answers.

In the End
"Ex-Factor" - Lauryn Hill

A few weeks or so went by after I'd cried my heart out to God at church. Knowing and believing that God wasn't going to let anything happen to me, I never lost faith. I continued to go to work every day because nothing would stop me from providing for my little prince. He was the highlight of my world, the one thing that brought me a source of unconditional and unlimited pure love. I loved this little boy far more than I could've ever conveyed in words. I can recall listening to the album "The Miseducation of Lauryn Hill," and it really helped heal me from the inside out. Two songs from that album stood out the most because I could relate to them on a deep level: Ex-factor & Zion. Ex-factor was a song about her coming to terms with the fact that no matter what she did, it would never be good enough for her man. The line that stands out the most is "Loving you is like a battle, and we both end up with scars" I felt those words deep down in my soul. My life and relationship started so innocent, so loving, so beautiful, and then out of nowhere. It spiraled out of control. The other song mentioned, called Zion, gave the words/lyrics to the feelings I felt inside about my motherhood journey. I used to cry while listening to both songs - cry, and pray. Now only one of those songs causes me to cry. Zion will forever be the soundtrack to the love for my son. Those tears are of love and joy.

Well, the day my prayers were answered was a day that I'll always remember. I was headed into work just like any other day in a car with deep scratches all over it because I had no money to fix my car. I had no money because I was the sole provider for myself and my son. I didn't get any assistance from the government or him. Can you imagine how embarrassing it was for me driving around in a car with a partial name carved into the door? People would always stare into my car or stare at me after seeing it. I'm sure secretly wondering what in the hell caused someone to do that to my car and why I was driving around with it like nothing was wrong. Unfortunately, I had no car insurance because I was barely able to provide for the bare basics. Anyway, this particular day the sun was shining, and birds were chirping. I was on my way to work, and when I got to work, my phone rang. On the other line was an investigator who told me that I didn't have to be afraid anymore because my ex had finally been picked up and would do some time for the awful things he'd done to me. I then got the ball rolling and applied for a three-year restraining order. It was effortless to convince a judge once I showed them the audio recordings of the crazy voicemails he would leave me. He called and left me almost 100 messages in one day.

So once the judge saw everything I'd gone through, the judge granted me a ten-year restraining order. I was finally free from my tormentor, although with mixed feelings. I knew that he truly had a good heart, and I kinda felt bad that he was going to jail. But ultimately, he was there because his actions caused him to deserve to be there, so my prayer was that he'd hopefully grow and learn from this experience so that when he got out, he would be better.

I went through so very much in that relationship, this was my first real relationship, and it was a roller coaster. I not only learned a lot, but I grew up a lot within that relationship too. I grew into a young, determined woman who would no longer accept abuse. I made myself a promise at that moment to never allow myself to be in another physically abusive relationship again, and I stuck to that. So if a guy were to exhibit any aggressive or controlling behaviors, I wouldn't even entertain it. Eventually, he was released from custody, and as time went by, he'd regained a lot of his old self back. While inside, he was officially diagnosed with his disorder and given medication. While on his medication, he was finally behaving fine, and after a while, I even felt comfortable allowing him to spend time with our son. He seemed to have grown up some while being away, and as long as he was in his right mind, I had no problem with him spending time with our son.

Years later, we were finally able to officially make peace. He had finally apologized for everything he had put me through, and I didn't even realize how much I needed to hear that until I heard it. That relationship was the worst experience of my life, so it felt really good for him to acknowledge it and apologize. I was happily in another relationship by this time, but it still gave me some much-needed closure for that phase of my life. I forgave him, and we remained in a good place until his untimely passing. Our son was only nine when his father passed away, but he loves & remembers his father for who he truly was inside, a genuinely good-hearted person. I never spoke badly about his father to him and always reminded him that he possessed all of the best traits that his dad had. He has his dad's smile, walk, and laugh. But more than anything, he has his dad's, good heart. I know you may be thinking, how can she still say that this man had a good heart after everything he put me through?! Well before his mental instability, his heart was one of the biggest and best things about him. He always showed love & respect to everybody and never showed any hate towards anyone. He wouldn't hurt a fly. Sadly, he was just dealt some unfortunate cards in life, which caused some shifts that he had very little control over. I am glad that he eventually got himself together. I am grateful that I was able to forgive him, and for us to be in a good peaceful place before he passed on. Ultimately he lives on through our son, who has ALL of his father's best traits.

∂   *Lesson Learned - There's nothing too hard for God*

Chapter 2

Relationships & Situationships

My Buddy
"Can't Help But Wait" - *Trey Songz*

After leaving my son's father, I was pretty much focused on just working and providing for my baby. I can remember my friend at work insisting on hooking me up with her son's father's friend. I wasn't really feeling it too much, but since I hadn't dated in almost a year, I felt like it was time to give it a try. At this time, I met my buddy. I call him my buddy because he was just that, a buddy, a friend, and someone I ended up dating exclusively. He and I had a really good rapport with one another and got along perfectly. He was Mr. Right in my eyes. He and I both had children the same age and a lot of other things in common. We could talk about anything and were great friends more than anything. I was happy in my relationship until I found out it wasn't a relationship.

After seeing each other exclusively for many months, I just naturally assumed that we were a couple. We spent so much time together, we went on dates like a couple and helped each other out as a couple. Hell, I was even waking up at 3:30 am and driving this dude to work as a "couple." Well, one day, I asked him to define what we had because I just wanted to be sure we were both on the same page "as a couple." Low and behold, he revealed to me that what we had was perfect, but he didn't want to put a title on it. That blew my mind because I couldn't understand the problem with proclaiming that we were in a relationship if we were only dealing with each other? He kept trying to explain that it was more because he was returning from school and didn't want to get in a relationship because relationships mess everything up, and what we had was going good. Well, yeah, it was going good, until then. After that bombshell, I started to feel like this wasn't in my best interest.

As much as I extended myself for him and as much time as we spent together, I could not be satisfied with us only being "buddies." So I did what any other person that was getting good at breaking up with people who no longer served her well, and I broke it off. It wasn't easy, but again, once my mind is made up, it is usually made up for good. Our situation was short-lived but long enough to leave a lasting impression on my heart. He and I remained friends who always referred to each other as "buddy" throughout the years. Our relationship didn't flourish into anything serious, but our friendship was unmatched. He was like my very best "male" friend, and we always stayed in touch and would talk for hours. There was just a special little bond between us that couldn't be broken no matter what. We stayed in touch, and I leaned on him for advice and him on me. Our lives took us in different directions over the years, he and I both ended up in other relationships (and marriages), but we always pretty much still stayed in touch. He was always going to be my buddy.

∂   *Lesson Learned - Mr. Right can sometimes be just Mr. Right now*

From Boyfriend To Grown Man
"Age Ain't Nothing But A Number" – Aaliyah

After ending my last situation, at nineteen years old, I met a man nine years older through mutual friends. Let's just call this my "Mature" relationship. He and I hit it off well, and he ended up moving in with me (without me asking) after a few months. It was kind of funny; he would come over and spend the night a few nights out of the week, and then one day, he just never left. Although we were nine years apart, I never felt like we were in two different spaces or on two different levels. I was always mature thinking and ahead of my time. So in this case, my age was just a number and not an indicator of anything. Plus, you know what they say, women are years ahead of men in maturity levels, so we probably were leveled out.

He was very good to me, but he stopped doing the things he did to attract me after a while. (You know how they do). We were together for about two years, and I can remember feeling like, "damn!? He just stopped all that love & affection I got in the beginning"! I wasn't very happy with how he fell off and made sure to tell him, but even though he said he'd improve, he never really did.

∂   *Lesson Learned - If they don't continue doing the things they did to get you, they don't deserve to keep you.*

Despite him not making much of an effort to change things, I was still all in. After all, I was only about twenty-one years old, so I was still green to relationships. Also, we didn't have any issues other than a few petty things. Such as he seemed to love his car more than he loved me, and he was cheap as hell (Frugal is what many prefer to call it), and he didn't like to do much. But I wasn't too concerned because we had a good thing going, and after my past, I was hesitant to leave. I didn't have any issues with abuse or mistreatment nor concerns regarding him cheating on me, he was also helpful with bills, and he even financed a car for me when I couldn't get approved alone. I felt like we were headed towards the aisle. I had strong feelings for him and believed we had a chance at a real future. I wanted a family, and I was determined to get one.

I guess the best way to describe our relationship would be easygoing and unproblematic. There wasn't any excitement, but it also wasn't anything wrong outside of him, not showing me his feelings. I didn't feel the love, and there was very little affection. Sadly, our relationship had become complacent. We had developed a routine of things we would eat, the TV shows we would watch, and the time we would go to bed. Life was pretty good for the most part. I had moved on from working at one hospital to a different one making more money. He was working a better job. My son was healthy and happy and spent a lot of time with his Dad's side of the family via his Aunt. I was blessed and didn't have much to complain about.

Let Go & Let God
"Shackles" - Mary Mary

Shortly after turning twenty-one, I began to get back into church heavily. You see, one of my older sister's husbands became a pastor of a church, so we all rallied around him and joined the church. During this time, I learned a lot more about God & began to grow closer to God. I can recall one particular quote that stood out to me and became my favorite. "Let go and Let God." That quote resonated with me and caused me to do some introspective thinking. I always had faith, and even more so after knowing and realizing that God had saved me from that last crazy relationship. So, I was very much in tune with trying to live my life better for God, and my brother's teaching of the word was always done phenomenally well. I learned so much under his leadership and just kept working to grow closer to God.

After a while, I was at a place where I wanted to do better, have better, and honor God better. I desired a husband, a man of God who would take good care of me and my heart. I wanted to feel like God blessed my relationship. At the time, my man wasn't into church, so that caused me a lot of concern, plus he seemed so complacent. I explained how I was feeling and told him that I no longer felt comfortable having pre-marital sex.

That was one of the scariest conversations ever because I didn't know how he would take it. The marriage thing wasn't new because he and I had previously had conversations about marriage. He knew without a doubt that what I wanted and desired was to be married and live happily ever after. But he was against going to church, and nothing I would say could make him change his stance.

We continued with our celibate relationship for quite a while before I finally decided that this wouldn't work for me either. I wasn't getting what I needed out of this relationship. I was much younger than him and less established, but I was settling for less than what I knew I deserved. I hung in there a little while longer, but I knew that this relationship's expiration date was near. I wanted what I wanted, and I didn't want to compromise on my happiness anymore.

I guess I'm a hopeless romantic because I always believed that someone was specially made out there for everyone. For me, I felt very strongly that my husband was out there somewhere, so I wasn't interested in wasting my time any longer. So I took my favorite quote ("Let go and Let God") to heart and found myself deciding to end my current and very serious relationship.

Once I decided that I didn't want to continue on this way, It didn't matter what feelings I still had for him, I knew that I needed to break up with him and move on with my life because somewhere out there, my husband was waiting. Was it hard? Absolutely, yes! I was so scared that I may make another mistake like I did in high school by breaking up a decent situation because I desired more. We see how that one ended up. I went back to my first boyfriend because the grass wasn't greener, and then that impacted my first relationship greatly. So you can only imagine the fear I had inside of "what if I'm not making the right choice?", "what if I am making the same mistake again and then decide later that I want him back?"

Sure, I had some conflicting thoughts about it. You never really know how something is going to turn out. It is very scary to step out on faith but I was a different person now, versus the young girl back then.

Here's the difference between the "me" in that first situation and the "me" now, NOW I had put my life in God's hands and trusted him to guide my decision. So this was a lesson learned that when it's time to go, go! Now, although I was leaving a relationship that wasn't bad, and it could backfire on me, I was very content in knowing that God had my back. I knew this decision was right because this time, I was ending things for very good reasons. I did not doubt my decision or my reasons - especially since one of those reasons was "to improve" my relationship with God, I knew that I'd be okay.

The Bittersweet End
"Half-Crazy" - Musiq Soulchild

This breakup was a bittersweet moment for me because this was a relationship that I'd been comfortable in. I didn't have a lot of experience at relationships until this point, so I grew up and matured a lot while in this one, and I was grateful for that. Considering what I had been through in my first relationship, this one was a very much welcomed stark contrast. I was very happy to be in a safe and secure relationship. They say everything happens for a reason, so I was ok with how things happened and progressed. I can't say for certain that I'd ever really reached that level where I felt like I was really in love, but it was the closest thing to it I'd ever experienced. Despite all of that, I stuck with my decision and left the relationship believing wholeheartedly that I would get what I wanted: a husband.

After the breakup, I stayed in church and kept it pushing. I was focused on working and providing for my son and I. We met up a few months or so after breaking up to get closure. I remember that day we stood on the corner and he and I kissed for the last time. I knew then that it was truly over, and I could rest my mind that I'd made the right decision. Not because the kiss was terrible, but because I felt a calmness overcome me as if God was comforting me and releasing my heart to truly move on. We also remained friends, speaking ever so often over the years. He eventually did marry and became the father of three little girls.

Chapter 3

Married Life

Bittersweet Lessons

How I Met My Husband
"Foolish" – Ashanti

I remember speeding down the freeway on my son's birthday. I was rushing to pick up some things for his party. Well, I ended up getting pulled over and issued a ticket. That ticket then caused me to have to go to traffic court in Hayward. I had never had a ticket before and didn't know the process, but I decided to try and get it taken care of. I can remember sitting in the courtroom, and the court attendant was a young black guy, but I didn't think anything of it. After my case was heard, I had to stand in a line to sign up for traffic school, and it was there that the guy from upstairs approached me. "Excuse me, do you mind if I give you my number?" Is what he said. I was not interested because I'd just left my last relationship, so I thought I'd hit him with a fastball. "Do you go to church"? Is what I asked. I already figured that he probably didn't, and that would throw him off, but to my surprise, he answered me by saying not only did he go to church, he was a long-standing member and also paid his tithes & offering. I can't lie and say I wasn't impressed at his quick answer/comeback because I was expecting my question to turn him away. So I let my guard down and gave him my number.

To say that our relationship moved fast is an extreme understatement!! It moved faster than a NASCAR! It's ironic because although I took his number, I neglected to call him for like two weeks. I just wasn't sure if I wanted to start another relationship situation yet. But I ended up bored one day and decided to call because what's the worst that can happen, right? *insert blank stare* Welp, the rollercoaster began in the first conversation. We talked for a good long time in our initial conversation, and I noticed that he talked a good game. He put on a great representative of himself and seemed like a nice guy, but during this time, I had a few prerequisites for the guy I wanted to be with and ultimately marry. There were ten things that were a must:

1. He needed to put God first
2. He had to be honest
3. He had to love kids
4. He wouldn't cheat (is loyal)
5. He had both a job & a stable living situation
6. Hadn't been to jail and didn't put his hands on women
7. He would have no baby mama drama
8. He'd have a good sense of humor
9. He'd be Intelligent
10. He should have a friendly & calm disposition

They say hindsight is 20/20, and boy oh boy, all the red flags and signs were there, and yet, I ignored them all. Let's say that of my list of ten requirements; he met about four and a half if that's even possible. Ha! And yes, I said half, and that was on number nine - go figure!

He had all the right things to say and was very good at making himself seem like a great guy. I can recall our long conversations on the phone, and he was really fun to talk to. I noticed that he found "creative" ways to boost himself up. For example, instead of saying he was a court attendant, he would say he was a bailiff. They are two different things, although similar, it wasn't a big deal to me; it was noted that he embellished. After he revealed to me that he played on a semi-pro football team, I was hesitant to talk to him further because, in my mind, athletes were all cheaters. I explained my feelings to him, and he assured me that cheating athletes were only a stereotype. I had doubts but decided to go on a date and see where things went. The date went well, and our relationship moved fast from there. I was celibate for a while until this point, so when things got hot and heavy after our date, I became weak and gave in. I can look back now and realize that there were better choices I should have made, but hey, I was young and dumb like many early twenty-year-olds.

We began spending lots of time together, and he would often say how much he liked me and could see himself marrying me. Uh oh... there go those magical words for me. From the moment those words left his lips, I had made my mind up and was convinced that this was my husband.

From the beginning, we were very much involved and inseparable. He never "officially" asked me to be his "girlfriend," but he didn't need to because we were conducting ourselves as such, so I knew that didn't need to be laid out and explained. But I want you to remember that part for later because it will be of importance. He lived in Hayward, and I lived in Oakland, which is less than about a fifteen-minute drive away from one another. One of the things that I can recall when we first began was that I'd asked him if he had any children, and he responded that he "kinda" had kids. I was thinking to myself, "Kinda?!" He then worded it that he had two kids but really just one. So now I am really confused, and I asked him how? Turns out, he had twin girls who were about eight months old at the time. Can you imagine my surprise? I was completely floored because he hadn't mentioned one word about having children of his own, on his own plus I wasn't sure what it means that this man has children so young. He explained to me that he and their mom were never an item and that he didn't find out about them until they were six months old. As it turns out, these girls' mother was extremely young, bitter, full of drama, and immature. So by now, as you can see, I had already broken several of my prerequisites lists.

∂   *Lesson Learned - You made those pre-reqs/requirements for a reason!! Do not settle!*

I kinda figured that the fact that he had kids so young was going to be a potential problem, and boy, was I right. It was weird to me because he never made any effort to see them. It wasn't like they lived out of state, they lived a few cities over, but he never seemed too concerned with them, and they never spent any time with him. I had a son of my own, so I could not tolerate dating a total deadbeat. I would repeatedly ask him about his children, and he had so many reasons and excuses for his behavior with the number one reason being he wasn't even sure if they were his kids. That was a shocker for me, but I didn't want to overstep too much. As time went on and we had our son, more and more time passed with him having little to no interaction with the twins, nor was he seemingly concerned about them, so I became concerned. It didn't help that their mom was a complete lunatic who had an affinity for drama and games.

Despite all of that, I still could not understand why he wasn't stepping up. I would often tell him that if you are their father, you need to do what you need to do to spend adequate time and love & support them. If that means taking their mom to court for partial custody, then so be it, I'll be here every step along the way. He had no reason not to fight for them, yet he didn't. This was indeed a red flag, and it was a big one that I should have never ignored because it showed how important fatherhood was to him.

I think I gave him a small pass once he admitted that he wasn't positive that they were indeed his children. But then I wondered, well, how come you haven't taken steps to find out?!?!? You see, this in itself was a whole other red flag. Not taking care of your business. It's hard for me to respect a person who doesn't handle business but instead lets the chips fall where they may. That was not the type of man I desired or needed in my life. I needed someone who solves problems and not accepts them! So, that was the beginning of what eventually lead to me developing a pattern within our relationship that he despised. I started handling shit myself, and he hated it.

Don't get me wrong, I'd give him an opportunity to handle something first, but I would handle it myself if he didn't. He grew to hate it so much, but after being disappointed so many times by what he wasn't doing, I felt like I had no other choice. So the beginning of this was when I finally convinced him to get a DNA test done. This was several years later into our relationship when I finally talked him into finding out if the girls were his. He had no idea that I'd already ordered a DNA test online. I ordered it from a reputable company online with good reviews, so when it came, I got him to request time with the girls, and he did. When the girls came over, I swabbed everybody's mouth! To me, it made no sense at all going through life, not knowing if your children were your children.

So it turns out, Once we got the results back, which took a few weeks, those babies who were by this time about four years old, were not his biological children. He was faced with the truth at this point, and when he confronted the mom, she already knew he wasn't their father and revealed that she was using him. The situation was very sad, but we were grateful for the truth.

Later within our relationship, this red flag bit me in the ass once I birthed our children. The first sign was during my pregnancies; he was helpful but not doting or even very appreciative. In time, we had two boys in addition to my first son, (whom he claimed as his own) who he barely did anything with. I was deeply disappointed in his lack of fathering traits. He loved our boys 100%, no denying that, but he was not really interested in everything that a father was. He wouldn't take them out to spend time with them; he didn't take them to play ball; he didn't teach them any sports; he didn't bond with them much. It was something that broke my heart and put a huge wedge in our relationship. I couldn't understand how a man who loved sports so much that he played well into adulthood wasn't the least bit interested in pouring into his sons so that they would be just as good if not better than him. Now don't get me wrong; he wasn't a terrible father. He just had a different idea when it came to parenting. He valued his presence more than his bond. As a little boy, he yearned for his father's presence for many years, so I think that he felt like his presence was enough. He was physically in the same house; he was always there physically to attend every game or event. Yes, they did eventually get into sports, but that was only after I once again took things into my own hands and signed them up myself. But yes, he was there for them cheering at every game, event, and even practices. I began thinking that much of that was so that he wouldn't have to hear my mouth if he did not show up, but the point is, he was always there. He was also big on discipline and respect, so he kept them in line as the disciplinarian. But, sadly, there was a big part missing within his relationship with our children. He approached fatherhood like a dictatorship. He missed showing his concern for their feelings, and he didn't prioritize the things that they needed long term instilled.

Uh Oh
"Crazy in Love" – Beyoncé

Okay, so let's go back a little bit to before we had the kids. Being so young (and dumb), the decision to sleep with this man on the first date was horrible. It was an awful decision, but it wasn't the worst part of the decision. What's even worse is that we didn't use any protection even though we both knew I wasn't on any birth control, plus I didn't even know him that well.

> ∂   *Lesson Learned – Thoroughly get to know anyone you give your body to if you don't want to regret it!*

I look back and realize how naive I was. I thought he was a good guy because he acted the part, and he said all of the right things. Any embellishments or inconsistencies that I noticed were quickly brushed under the rug because the good outweighed the bad. Not to mention, the man told me that he saw marriage in our future.

Well, what happens next shouldn't be much of a surprise. Next thing I know, BAM! I'm pregnant, and by the next thing, I mean exactly two months later after we met. So here I am pregnant, and although he and I are both kinda nervously excited about this news, it was just so damn very fast. We barely knew each other after only two months. We discussed it, and I realized that he seemed way more excited than shocked or nervous like me. There was no doubt that he wanted this for us and wanted us to be together. At the time, we both were pretty stable in our lives, so we openly accepted that we would be bringing a child into this world.

I can remember having intuitive doubts about him very early on, but I brushed them off with things moving so fast. I never once prayed and asked God to confirm if this were my husband because I was almost sure he'd tell me no. One day, however, I could no longer just brush my doubts off because when I went to one of my doctor visits during my pregnancy, the doctor informed me that I'd somehow contracted chlamydia and E-Coli. Insert the WTF face here!! The wind had been knocked out of me at this point because I knew there was only one way this could have happened. My man was out there cheating. So, of course, I immediately confronted him. Once confronted, he began to explain that he wasn't currently sleeping with anyone else, but he had a few months before we got together. So he convinced me that the STDs had to have come from his previous sexual relationship. Since we were only a few months in (*See the last Lesson Learned and then insert eye-roll emoji and face palm emoji*), I felt like it was reasonable. More than anything, I realize that that's what I wanted and needed to believe because I was pregnant, dammit, so this had to work. Plus, he was my husband, right?!

As time went on, our relationship continued to grow and progress. We ended up moving in together a few months later. I can remember that I started having strong suspicions and inner feelings based on things I'd been noticing. His demeanor would change often; he wasn't always completely truthful. Also, he seemed to never really want to leave his phone around me, I mean, wherever he went, that phone went. I'd catch him in little dumb, unnecessary lies. Sometimes he would even go MIA for hours and have every excuse in the world when he came back around. I didn't want to believe the inevitable because after all, we were pregnant, and this was supposed to be my prince charming, my Ken doll, my chance at happiness, right? Plus, I had enough to deal with because my pregnancy was shaping up to be complicated. I was extremely sick all of the time, and instead of gaining weight, I was losing weight. I couldn't keep food down and felt miserable the whole first half of the pregnancy. I leaned on him a lot to help me, and he did somewhat always stay available to help me. But he didn't seem to appreciate or respect the fact that I was carrying his baby. You know how you see the movies or shows when the man is extra careful, treating you as fragile and carrying precious cargo. He didn't make me feel any extra special than before, and I saw that as a problem but forced myself to get over it.

So here I am big and pregnant, not feeling appreciated or special and having suspicions. So there was this one day that I couldn't resist snooping. Well, you know what they say, don't go looking for nothing, because you probably won't like what you find. Yeah, yeah, but the bible says seek, and ye shall find soooo I decided to take that route. Welp, I guess it's true what "they" say because what do you know, my suspicions were correct. I found out he was cheating, and I was completely devastated!!! This was only my third serious relationship in life, and it was the second time I'd been cheated on. The difference between the two, though, was that my first boyfriend admitted to the act because he felt guilty about it. See, with Boyfriend #1 (My son's father), He cheated early in our relationship, but the guilt was eating him up inside, so he told me exactly what happened in detail and apologized for his decision. He regretted his decision, and he vowed never to do it again. The fact that he'd told me on his own made a huge impact on me. I respected that! To my knowledge, he didn't do it again. This time though, things were a lot different in this relationship, especially since I'd found out on my own after snooping.

He'd left his emails open on our desktop computer, so I scrolled through looking for anything that stood out. Well, it turns out he was still seeing his ex, or I should say the manly looking chick who he was with before me. I saw an email from her saying she'd enjoyed their last tryst. So apparently he had been cheating during our whole relationship because she had no clue he had moved on into a new relationship or had a baby on the way. How do I know? Because I called her to get to the bottom of things. You know, woman to woman *insert another eye roll* I remember thinking about how he had lied to me, he told me he wasn't doing anything with anyone else when I contracted those STDs, and he was! I was so damn angry. Angry with him but also mad at myself. I can remember thinking to myself, how in the hell did I allow myself to be so stupid to get involved with this type of guy and situation? I already had one son and was currently pregnant with another, and the one thing I didn't want was to ever be a chick who had multiple kids by multiple fathers and not be with either one of them. No, I wanted a husband because I knew that I was wife material.

With that in mind, I believe that when I heard his explanation, I allowed myself to believe what I wanted to believe instead of what I should have logically believed. It was far better to believe him than the alternative. His explanation was comical, wait for it... he said that we never really became an "official" couple because he'd never "officially" asked me to be in a relationship. So he believed that gave him an excuse to date around because we weren't "official".

Everyone take a second here and think about this. He felt as if he and I were both still single to date because he never "officially" asked me to be his "girlfriend". Tuh! Here I am all into this man, thinking he was the one, thinking he was serious about marriage with me. I mean, I was already pregnant with his baby, and we lived together, so in my mind, we had already bypassed a lot of those steps. I couldn't believe that he acted like we were not officially a couple, even though we did all the "official" things that couples do and were officially pregnant. I was like WTF?!

Now, do you all remember how I told you a few pages back to "remember this part for later", yea well as you can see, the BS I'd just experienced was a result of not having that clarity? I assumed instead of getting real clarity on the status of our relationship from his perspective.

∂ *Lesson Learned – Always get clarity about where your relationship stands or if you are even IN one instead of assuming*

If he's serious about you, his answer to this question will reflect that. We continued living together after he apologized and declared that he and I understood our relationship now. So I decided to forgive him and move past it for our baby boy to come. I wanted to have a family and not just be a "baby mama".

I had seen and noticed so many warning signs and red flags at this point in our relationship. But I conveniently ignored a lot of them because I was determined for this relationship to work. I didn't take the little white lies serious or the inconsistencies or even the many character & personality flaws that were outright terrible. He was also overly aggressive at times and didn't quite know how to talk to people effectively. But I kept holding on to that hope deep down inside that this was my guy. He was my chance at the life I knew I wanted and deserved, so I pretty much ignored all of that.

∂ *Lesson Learned - Do not ignore red flags!! I ignored several red flags, and then I would make excuses for others.*

The one thing I would not or could not ignore or accept was cheating, though. So his defense of we was never really officially together, even though I was already pregnant by him, was accepted with a grain of salt by me. I remember feeling relieved that the cheating experience had happened in my young naivety because I felt like now he had learned a lesson in making this mistake and knew not to do it again.

I believed that we had gotten it out of the way early in our relationship. The red flag was replaced with a white one by me. I didn't want to be at odds. I wanted to be a family. I mean, he did vow never to do it again, and I witnessed him cry real tears and open up and share with me about his past traumas. I was sure that he had changed. So yes, I decided that I would forgive him, and we could move on. After all, this man loved me, right? I'd watched him cry real tears over potentially losing me, so he had to love me, right? So after being cheated on, I stayed in the relationship believing he'd changed.

∂ *Lesson Learned- Crocodiles cry real tears too*

I'm Out
"So Gone" – Monica

As time progressed and for the first few years of our relationship, we broke up and got back together several times. There were a few more times that he was caught lying about females in one way or another. Each time I felt myself drifting further away. I felt like he had disrespected our relationship, but I never had solid proof of actual cheating. I remember being so insecure about our relationship. I didn't fully trust him and felt like I couldn't give my all to him like I wanted to because of what he'd done. I remember whenever we went out in public, I'd wonder just how many of the women we encountered were women he had been with? I was beginning to see that he was a male whore before our situation, so I was side eyeing any woman he seemed to know or see in passing. It was very uncomfortable being that insecure in our relationship, and whenever I tried to express my feelings, he made me feel like I was crazy.

We were living together initially when our son was born and had a nice apartment. Then you are going to believe what happened next. (Yes, I left out the "not" part purposefully). He got caught cheating again. How did I catch him, you wonder? Well, it wasn't hard at all because the silly girl kept calling our house and playing on the phone. When I finally chatted with the girl, she admitted that they were fooling around and that he was lying to me. I decided to try and get some proof, so I asked her to go on a three-way call with him and me. She didn't tell him that I was on the line, and she called him and baited him into admitting that they were fooling around. Not only that, when she asked him if they could see one another again soon, his response was "he didn't know because she had made things harder for him to sneak away after playing on our phone". I had heard what I needed to hear at that point and revealed myself on the phone call. He was caught red-handed and couldn't figure out what to say or do, so he hung up. I remember I was at work in the office, and one other person was sitting next to me in the office. I didn't know how much she had heard, but at that point, I didn't care because I was utterly fuming! I felt like my head was on fire and would explode unless I did something. After hearing the proof with my ears, I was completely heartbroken and devastated, but more than anything else, I was pissed. Our whole life was a lie. My fairytale was turning into a shitshow!

I decided to investigate even further. After hacking into his computer emails and his Myspace, I also hacked into his cell and work phones' voicemails and heard messages from other women.

I just knew he wasn't cheating with all of these women, especially these older ones, right? I mean, some of them were well into their 50s. (Which isn't old, but we were only around 23 & 25) After getting into his voicemail and his work voicemail, it was confirmed that he was not just cheating, he was out there **cheating** cheating! I mean, it was crazy! He was messing with all kinds of women. Not to mention, he seemingly had no preference. They could be young, old, big, small, or ugly, so I was done.

It was clear that this dude had a problem. I had all of the proof I needed. I was so very hurt and angry that I knew I wouldn't ever be able to get over this, so I had no problem throwing up the deuces and leaving him. But first, I bagged up all of his shit, and I drove to his job and dumped all those bags out onto the sidewalk right in front. I then made a phone call to him at his desk and told him his shit was outside, and then I drove away. I learned later that by the time he got downstairs, people had started pilfering through his clothes and shoes, so he was thoroughly embarrassed and pissed. He was so pissed that he decided to get me back by throwing some of my prized possessions into the dumpster when he got home. I wasn't home at the time, so I didn't even realize it at first. I was baffled that this fool had the audacity to respond in such a way to my hurt when he was the cause of all of this happening in the first place. So you cheat and break my heart, and then when you get mad at how I react, instead of acknowledging the hurt you caused, or try to make things right, you continue to do dumb and disrespectful shit. I was done!

> ∂ *Lesson Learned - If he cheats on you and then is narcissistic enough to retaliate or make excuses instead of taking ownership - run, Sis!!!*

I moved out and got my own apartment, and we went our separate ways. Our son was barely one years old if even that. After our relationship ended, we decided to work on being good co-parents for our son. Strangely enough, we seemed to get along better as co-parents. He would come by to see his son periodically, and it was working out well. He also would always try to convince me that he had changed and was over the cheating thing, but I didn't buy it. He didn't let up. He kept trying to convince me that we were better off together instead of apart. After a while, I got weak, and my defenses were broken down because I began to consider giving my family another chance.

We were dating other people off and on, but after dating other people for a while, I guess I finally got weak and gave in. We ended up reconnecting and got back together again. Deep down inside, I was still dealing with the insecurity about having babies with no father or relationship, so I felt led to try and force it to work. I guess we couldn't shake the love we had for one another. Well, let me be honest. I still, at this point, wasn't even sure what love truly was or what it felt like, so I didn't know if it was love that I was feeling or something else. It seemed to me that I must have been in love with him because I kept finding myself back with him. But, I didn't feel like I was truly in love with him. I just logically decided that this must be love since we told each other that. I also thought about the fact that the cheating instances had me feeling like he broke my heart, so that meant that this had to be love, right?

Listen to how crazy I was. At one point after we got back together, he was living with another woman. After our break up, the back story was that it was hard for him to afford a place on his own, so he was doing a lot of couch surfing until his coworker (who happened to be a woman) offered up her place. I didn't have a problem with his living situation at first, although we were back together, I wasn't ready to go back to living together just yet. Plus, the lady he lived with was a slightly older and chunky coworker that he assured me was only a platonic friend who had a couch for him to sleep on. He also acknowledged to me that she was very unattractive and wouldn't ever be his type. I believed him, although my intuition started tingling. After we reconnected, I could tell that she was more invested in their situation being more than a platonic friendship, and I tried to tell him that she was interested in him. I could tell because when he and I were on the phone cupcaking, she'd always find a reason to have something to say to him. When I went to drop our son off to him, I finally was able to see/meet her. She was pissed that I'd shown up there unannounced, so that, of course, made me side-eye his platonic claims.

Then, when I thought about how unattractive she was, I dismissed my concerns because I didn't think he was interested.

∂   *Lesson Learned - Men will cheat with anyDAMNbody, so don't let the looks fool you.*

I knew that she was indeed interested in him, but you know how some men are, blind to the facts. He always denied there being anything there, and eventually, he moved out of there and moved back in with me. We had officially got back together again. I never found out if they were sleeping together or not, but I knew one thing if she got her way, they would have been.

Jumping the Broom
"Let's Get Married" - Jagged Edge

Once we finally rekindled our relationship, I was sure this time was going to be different. I felt like we both had dipped our toe in the water and realized that what was out there didn't compare to being a family. So guess what, a short time later, guess what we did? We got married. Yes! It had finally happened. The moment I had been waiting for since I was a little girl. I can recall the days before when we went to get our marriage license and feeling so eager. I was so happy that I was finally getting married. I was excited to be a wife and to call someone my husband. I couldn't wait to walk around with a wedding ring on. It felt like such an accomplishment to me. I was very happy to get married finally, but it was bittersweet because we didn't have that traditional wedding as I'd fantasized about. We also didn't have a honeymoon or anything like that. He never really even actually proposed to me. Our marriage came to be due primarily because we attended my brother's church, and several other young married couples were there. At one point, there were like two or three couples who all got married after church within a few months, so it was sort of a "thing" within our church. Plus, I valued my relationship with God & church. I had very strong feelings that I needed to repair my relationship with God and decided in that instant that I wanted to have a husband, NOT a boyfriend.

Since getting back together, we were smooth sailing in our relationship. I didn't have to encounter any more cheating problems, but I was back to being celibate because I wanted to do right by God. I recalled how he would always say that he knew that he would never cheat on his wife once he got married. I asked him why he felt that way, and he said it was something that he just knew deep inside. When our son was a little over 18 months old, I wrote out all of the pros and cons of us getting married and logically presented it to him. He agreed that it made sense for us to do it, and we discussed our decision with our pastor and set a date. We were so young, and we didn't have much money, so we decided to have a small church wedding, and a real wedding would happen later. I was okay with waiting for my big day. After all, I'd already felt like I had the prize. I still wanted my dream wedding, though.

∂   *Lesson Learned - If a man is truly ready to marry you, he will ask you!*

One thing that always used to nag at me about my relationship was that we didn't seem to have God in it. Sure, we both went to church, but for him, it was 100% for appearances. He didn't do anything else outside of attending. What I mean by that was, he never prayed, he never talked about God, didn't know any scriptures, and wasn't following some of those commandments too closely. We had been together for quite a while and attended church every Sunday but had never even prayed together. I had never once heard him pray, not for me or anyone else. I didn't see him pursuing or cultivating a genuine relationship with God, and I didn't feel like God was truly telling me that this was the guy for me. I never once prayed and asked God to guide me because I didn't think he would confirm that I was in the right relationship deep down inside. Since I wanted to be married so badly, I neglected to make sure that God sent it. I was so determined to make this thing work that I didn't want to see things in any other way. Boy, oh boy, that was a huge learning lesson in my life

∂   *Lesson Learned - Always seek confirmation and guidance from God on your relationship.*

After getting married, we began a new chapter in our life together. Remember the coworker lady he used to live with previously? Well, this heffa decided to express hurt and anger towards him once the word got around, and she found out we were married. She told him that she was disappointed because she wanted things to progress between them. All I could do was think to myself, I knew it! I knew I had that intuitive feeling that she was interested in more than a platonic relationship, and of course, him being naive or stubborn, he didn't or couldn't see what I saw until after she finally revealed the truth. That intuitive feeling I had about her proved to be true.

∂   *Lesson learned - Always listen to your intuition. It's usually always right!*

What Is This?
Unappreciated – Cherish

The first year was the worst year ever in our marriage. People had warned us that the first year of marriage would be rocky, but I never imagined it would be this damn bad. I was not a happy camper that first year, and we almost didn't make it. Not only did he get caught cheating again about two months in, but he also was a total asshole. He only saw things from his perspective and did not seem to care about my feelings at all. He was so selfish and just plain ole stupid. I was completely disappointed with my marriage. The girl he cheated with was none other than the same chick. Ms. Manly Ex. She just kept popping back up. I didn't feel honored or cherished by my husband, and I was totally over it. I was ready to throw the towel in because his true colors were truly being revealed. I knew that I wasn't being loved correctly, and I had reached my breaking point. I naively believed that he would never cheat once we took vows and now look. He was just a liar at this point, and I couldn't believe anything he said. I'd decided that this wasn't what I wanted for myself and that I'd had enough. So I expressed to him that this was the end of our relationship, and surprisingly he fought and fought hard to get me to stay. He refused to give up on us, and he cried, begged, and pleaded to show me that he had changed. He even suggested counseling, which he previously scoffed at, to help fix what was wrong. He seemed so sincere, unlike any of the other times before. This time was different. He was fighting hard to keep his family together, so this time I knew that there would be some changes. Eventually, we got through it, after all, this was my husband, and I was the chosen one, right?! Those other women were the losers, and I was the winner. What I didn't realize back then was that the prize was no prize at all, and this kind of "prize" was slowly killing me inside.

We went to counseling at least four or five different times throughout our marriage. It literally would take both the counselor and me to explain things over and over before he would finally see or acknowledge the error in his ways and how his actions were the cause of the reactions he received on an everyday basis. He was a walking, living & breathing narcissist, and it showed in so many of his actions. It was almost surreal to see how his mind could never connect the dots on how he was wrong on so many levels until an outside person with no ties could explain it to him. So with counseling, we stayed together, and eventually, things improved.

Over time, he and I had both learned to "accept" our marriage for what it was. When I say "accept," you can go ahead and replace that with "settle."

What do I mean by that? Well, I had learned to accept that he wasn't going to be that fairytale husband I'd dreamed about, he was not very reasonable in his thought processes, and he was overly aggressive and mean at times. He also wasn't much more than just a disciplinarian to our boys. I used to joke that he was pretty much an in-home deadbeat dad. He wouldn't do much of anything with our boys. He didn't spend much time with them or take them out to play any sports. The kids were mostly afraid of him because he was always ruling like a dictator. He didn't tolerate much of anything, and I would often have to remind him to take it easy. I would remind him that just as he hated how his grandmother treated him, he needed to consider how he was treating our kids. No matter how many times I tried to get him to improve in parenting, he kept doing it his way. He would lighten up sometimes because he didn't want to deal with me coming down on him or my attitude, but for the most part, he was always acting like a dictator to our kids.

I longed for more... but I accepted. He had also learned to accept that I wasn't the most affectionate female and that I didn't have that nurturing mothering spirit he desperately wanted and needed for his ego. No matter how hard I tried, that nurturing mothering spirit would only come out for my boys. I was affectionate enough, in my opinion, but honestly, because I didn't feel completely safe in our "love," I never could fully get to the level that he wanted or needed from me. I realized that each time he hurt me, my love meter would decrease in capacity. It wouldn't ever be able to reach the heights that it once had ever again. I tried explaining that to him, and he never seemed to get it. I loved him with the full amount that I was able to scrounge up - it seemed.

When our son was about four, we decided that we wanted to try for a girl. I stopped my birth control with the hopes of getting pregnant, and shortly after doing that, it happened. We were both very happy and excited about this pregnancy, as this would be the first child born on purpose and in wedlock. Well, with my pregnancy, I felt like strides had been made and that our relationship was finally in a nice safe place. I was finally living the life that I'd imagined: married, with a two-income, two-car household, pregnant and glowing and eager for the future. I was quite disappointed with the way he treated me during pregnancy, though. Once again, I expected him to dote over me and make me feel like the world was mine. You know how you see those guys on the tv who bend over backward for their pregnant wives and stay ready for any opportunity to make life easier for the woman carrying their child. Yeah, this wasn't that. Instead, he acted like it wasn't anything special to him. This should have been another sign for me to take heed to, but I kept missing them (aka ignoring them) as often as they came.

∂ Lesson Learned - Again! Do not ignore the signs, aka "red flags."

Ultimately I had an okay pregnancy until about a month before I was due to give birth. I found out that my husband had been miscommunicating with other women. Although nothing was established as proven as him having an actual affair, the fact alone that he felt it was okay to have new female friends unbeknownst to me was a blow. I was so upset that I'd broken up with him WHILE still pregnant. I was ready to get off of this emotional roller coaster. I can recall talking it out with my sister-cousin and my friends and just mulling over how I could leave. He had threatened not to pay the rent if I kicked him out, so I had to be sneaky and find his cash to get the rent paid for the next month. I don't even remember how but we eventually made up (looking back on it now, I realize that I was very much addicted to the breakup/makeup cycle), but things began to improve, and I gave birth to our second son on September 5th, 2007. The first few weeks were a blur.

Juggling three children was a huge adjustment. Things were going pretty good, or so I thought. After having the baby, I was struggling a lot with finding time for myself. You see, I loved hanging out with my friends and sisters and welcomed any and every opportunity to do so. I had been on a few cruises and several mini girls trip over the past few years and had caught the travel bug. My husband didn't usually mind. It was a way for us to get some time apart so we could miss one another. I can recall coming back from one of my girls' trips in one particular instance, and I was so surprised by my hubby deciding to makeover our bedroom. He had completely cleaned and organized our room, and even bought a new comforter set. When I got home, the room was all nice, and he had candles and everything, it was sweet. He could be sweet when he wanted to be, and he was always very loving to me when we were on good terms.

The Ultimate Betrayal
"Stranger In My House" – Tamia

Family life was filled with a lot of mini issues and was hard at times, but nothing could prepare me for what happened next. He committed the ultimate betrayal. He'd now done the worst thing I could imagine. It was revealed to me on November 28th, 2007. Yes, I remember the exact date things shattered; it wasn't hard since this also happened to be the date to our 3rd wedding anniversary.

On my anniversary, 11/28/2007, I received a direct message from an account on my Myspace page belonging to a lady that my husband worked with at the nightclub. This particular girl I had already been warned about by other people at the club they both worked at. He was a bouncer, and she was a cocktail waitress, and one time when I came up there, the other waitress pulled me to the side and told me to watch her because she expressed interest in my husband. I asked him about it, and he, of course, denied anything of the sort. One day, I was at the club hanging out with my sister, and I noticed that this waitress girl kept going over to him and talking to him, so I made sure to look and pay attention. I can remember she was telling him something in his ear, and when she saw me looking, she smirked then walked away. I immediately went over to him and confronted him about why another woman is in his face. I was pissed, and he kept trying to downplay it and made it seem like I was crazy because nothing was going on. Now fast forward to the day, my life was turned upside down, and I am reading a message from this same girl detailing to me the extent of their ongoing almost two-year affair. She had details and receipts to back up what she was telling me, so I knew it was real. I can't even describe to you the feelings I had inside of me having read that. Here I was learning that my husband, whom I believed was faithful and honoring me, and our marriage was a fraud. Everything I'd believed about our union turned out to all be a lie. If ever there was a time where I truly felt like the rug was being pulled from under me, it was this exact moment. I couldn't breathe... I couldn't think or formulate thoughts. I just sat there and read it over and over again until the tears began to fall.

I am sure that many women can relate to the heartache you experience after realizing that everything you believed up until this point was a complete lie. Every touch, every "I Love You," every moment of concern, was now questionable. How can you possibly say you love me, you care for me? Do you respect me? You honor me as your wife if you are betraying me, my trust, and my heart. Once the details were revealed, I felt utterly and completely broken. I had been so damn stupid. This woman had been in my face, I'd met her, yet my husband still had no problem playing me in such a disrespectful way.

Oh, but that isn't even the worst part. What is worse is that she also revealed how he had brought her to our house, and he slept with her in our bed and that they never used condoms. With the details she provided, I was able to put two and two together and realized that the time I came home to the bedroom being made up so nicely was really because he had brought another woman over to our house and into our bed. I was completely devastated. Our marriage wasn't the best, but it also wasn't the worst and had improved so much that I truly didn't see this coming. The truth is, I can look back now and say I absolutely should have seen this coming with all of the things that lead up to it, but I didn't. I had never been hurt this bad in my life. I can remember just crying all the tears I had until the tears wouldn't fall anymore. I had no tears left. It felt like my heart had completely shredded. When I confronted him, he went back into formation, being tearfully apologetic. He cried real tears, begged, and pleaded, and assured me that it wasn't how it sounded. He was trying everything and saying anything to convince me, but I wasn't going for it this time. This time I was **DONE** done.

At this moment, I felt my heart turn cold. I had lost all respect for this man. I couldn't believe that I was in this situation and especially right after having a baby. A baby that we planned for together. Our son was only a few months old. I felt so defeated, but I also felt so strongly about leaving this relationship. You see, I was never the type to feel like I needed a man or like I was desperate to keep a man, so I knew that I did not have to put up with this bullshit. I was done. He kept doing and saying everything in his power to try and change my mind, but there was nothing he could do or say. This time I was truly done. I told him point-blank that I would never be able to love him in the way a wife should, so it was pointless for him to make me stay. I assured him that I knew myself better than anybody in this world, and I knew there was absolutely no way that my love would return full throttle, ever again. He still wanted to try and refused to give up, but I was done. I can remember feeling so embarrassed. I couldn't believe that I'd allowed myself to be played like that, so I ended our marriage at that point.

Although I was completely done, I wasn't in a position financially to pick up and leave. Plus, I had a newborn and needed as much help as possible. So we stayed in the same house but as strangers. After a while, I even began to flirt around and even date other men. I figured, why not?!? He had been dating throughout our whole marriage, seemingly. Because I had no respect for my husband, I didn't feel like I was doing anything wrong by dating. I mean, why not if our relationship was over? Sure we were still living together, and he was actively trying to get me back, but I was done. So I ultimately put a plan in place to use him being there as an opportunity for me to save up my money, and once I saved up enough money, I was going to throw up the deuces and move out. I had everything all figured out. I just needed time to pull it all together.

Life was miserable, as you can probably imagine. I despised this man but had to hide it from our children. I didn't want anything to disrupt my boys' world, so I gritted my teeth and stayed put doing all the things a mother should do. I wasn't doing anything wifely, and barely had any words for my husband. I just concentrated on being the best mom I could be to our boys. Raising little black boys in this world is hard enough. They will surely encounter so many obstacles because of the color of their skin. When your skin is the weapon they see, it is impossible not to be seen as a threat. One of the reasons I struggled internally with my decision to leave was because I knew that raising them without a father would be setting them up for even more hurdles as young black men. Being a mom who has always felt like your children's well-being should come before anything else, it was difficult for me to choose me.

During this time, I kept working on saving money, and he kept working on trying to win me back. Months and months had passed, and I can recall one day just collapsing in tears. I collapsed in our bedroom and just cried and cried and cried. He was shocked and very concerned because it seemingly had come out of nowhere. I was crying because I was conflicted, so very conflicted. I didn't know what I was supposed to do. I didn't know if God was telling me to leave or to stay. I laid on the floor and cried and refused to move or get up. He eventually began to cry, too, and we cried together. It was like some sort of purge was happening. I can't explain what happened inside of me, but I remember being tired. I was tired of feeling like this. Tired of feeling like a failure, like I couldn't have the life I wanted to live. I wanted my life back on track, and I wanted my family to work out, so at that moment, I decided to give it one last try.

After finally finding the will to work things out, we went to counseling again, and I began to work hard at forgiveness and moving forward. He was open to anything, and everything; not only were we going to counseling, but I also had passcodes and everything else. For me to be comfortable, I needed everything to be 100% transparent. I needed full access to his phone, his accounts, and everything in between. He freely gave me access to it all, and that went a long way in working on trusting again. I think back on this decision to try again, and I wonder if it was right or not, given the ultimate result. My answer is always conflicting because I feel like I made the decision that I felt was right at the time, and it did yield some positive changes and results. But, the one thing I didn't know or consider was that you couldn't change a person's character or fix what is broken inside of another person. They have to be willing to do that all on their own. If that isn't done, no matter how much time passes by, they are bound to fall back into that same routine at some point.

∂   *Lesson Learned - You cannot fix what is broken inside of another person; only they can do that!*

High Hopes
"Wishful Thinking" - Vivian Green

I can honestly say that I saw a huge difference in our relationship this time around. He was serious about making things right, and he showed it in his actions. He was always home with us, and when he wasn't around, his whereabouts were never questioned. One year flew by, and it was almost like celebrating sobriety; he was one year clean and clear from cheating. Two years went by, and then three and then four... next thing you know, seven years went by, and there were NO more incidents of cheating of any kind. I had no more problems with him entertaining female friends. I had no doubts about where he was or what he was doing when I wasn't around. I had regained trust, and our relationship had somehow survived.

I don't even fully know how we got through it because it was certainly one of the hardest things I've ever had to overcome. We had been through probably about four counselors, several churches and pastors, and a lot of family and friend advice during those years. Most of the time, everyone was encouraging us to work through our issues and stay together. Everyone loves Black Love, right? We need to see more of it; we need to have couples stay together so that people know it truly is possible. Plus, our boys deserved to have a two-parent home, something he and I both never had. So although I never really gained back that full amount of love and respect, I stayed. I wasn't very happy with everything that had transpired, but I stayed. I wasn't necessarily sad either; it wasn't like I was miserable within the renewed relationship; actually, it was quite the contrary.

Over these years, this man had done a complete 180 and shown that he loved me more than I ever thought possible. He was a very doting and affectionate husband who loved the ground I walked on. I had a husband who would do pretty much anything for me, and kill anyone with his bare hands if they were trying to hurt me. He was super overprotective over me, and I loved it. I think I loved that protectiveness because growing up, I didn't have the consistency of a father or big brothers or any other males around to give me that protectiveness. So I think that secretly I yearned for it, and it made me feel loved. I was pretty content with our marriage, and I was proud that we had turned things around. As crazy as it sounds, I did grow to fully trust him again. They say once trust is broken. It can never be returned; well, that wasn't true because I lived in the opposite of that truth. It took a lot of work and a lot of prayers, but it happened. I can recall when people would pose relationship questions such as: Can you trust after betrayal? Do men ever stop cheating? Can relationships overcome cheating betrayals? I was an advocate for the fact that things can and do change when a person wants to, grows up, and commits to.

I knew my husband loved me more than anything, and I knew that he knew that this relationship would be over if I ever caught him cheating again. So I trusted in that and trusted him to make the right choices. I can recall when he would tell me the stories and give me vivid details of how women would approach him, and he'd perfected turning them down. He was very proud of himself for being able to avoid temptation so easily. In some instances, he would tell me how he would even pull out his phone and brag about me by scrolling through the photos of me on his phone. He was proud of his wife, and he let everybody know it. There were even times when mutual friends would vouch for him and brag how he represented me and our marriage well out there. He was on his best behavior, and I was glad about it.

As more time went by, I realized that our relationship was good, but it was still missing that optimal level of love & respect from a wife to a husband. Yes, I had forgiven and moved on, but I still could not allow my heart to open up fully and love freely. Affection improved, communication improved, and trust improved, but I was still struggling to feel unconditional love and desire. I often would pray about it because I didn't know what else to do. I knew that his past discretions were why I was holding back, so I tried my best to forgive and move forward. But my love hadn't yet returned to the place it had been, and I knew deep down inside that it never would.

I began to bug him about us saving up and having a real wedding. Mostly because I felt cheated, it was sad enough that I was married without ever actually having been proposed to, but I also was married and never actually had a real wedding. I felt in my heart that renewing our vows would be instrumental in us starting over. I knew that I would have better luck with re-gaining all of the love and respect if I felt like we were starting from a clean slate. A vow renewal would be the perfect way to trick my heart & mind into action so that I could feel unconditional love again. It would mean that we were recommitting ourselves to one another, forsaking all others, and inviting God to take over. So I kept bugging him about it and explaining to him how important it was for me. He wasn't against it, but just like everything else, he didn't move one muscle to make it happen or even seem concerned with making it happen. He had big issues with my level of love & affection towards him, but he didn't seem too interested in doing what I felt was needed. So we just kept it moving and simply existing together in our marriage.

Then the year 2016 happened. 2016 Is a very significant year in our marriage because this year, things started to feel different.

"2016"
"Emotional Rollercoaster" - Vivian Green

I remember very clearly the feeling I had. I started to get that intuitive feeling that something wasn't 100% right. Our marriage was stable. We had minor disagreements and arguments as usual, but it wasn't anything crazy. By this time, I fully understood that marriage was like riding on a roller coaster. You will experience many highs and many lows, and no, you will not always feel happy or in love. Marriage is about commitment and deciding to stay together, no matter what. But I still had a bad feeling. Ladies, you all know the feeling I speak of because it's undeniable. The feeling is to have an in-depth knowledge of something without knowing…aka intuition. I had this feeling and couldn't shake it, so I began to snoop around. I hadn't done this in years because I hadn't felt any concerns or need to, and I hate even having to stoop to that level. But I went ahead, and I began to snoop.

I also began to watch and pay attention to his habits. A change in habits or behavior is one of the first signs that something is going on with your mate. I noticed he had an attitude like he didn't give a damn a lot more towards me lately. Usually, he hated it when I was mad at him. He hated the awkward silence or tension when we were not vibing and would relent and work to resolve things between us. I noticed that this wasn't happening anymore as of lately. So I began to note when he was coming home from working security on the weekends, and I noticed some nights he was coming home later than usual. He would get off work at 2 am and usually by the time they paid him, and he drove home, it would be around 3 am. He was now coming in after four, and he didn't think I knew because I acted like I was asleep. Usually, I actually would be fast asleep when he came home and would stay asleep even after he got in bed. But I'd started staying up and paying attention to the Life360 app, which gives details of your family's whereabouts at any given time. Sidenote: Our family has had this app on all of our phones for quite some time. It is to make sure you know where your family is at all times. When I first introduced this app, he wasn't too thrilled about it, but he relented after explaining to him that I wasn't trying to spy. I only wanted our family to remain connected and to be safe. Well, fast forward to now, and I now needed to use it to spy.

You've got to be a special kind of stupid if you'd try and cheat when you know your whereabouts can be tracked, So I wasn't expecting to find anything. But, I noticed he was going somewhere else after working the clubs, and of course, I assumed that it was connected to a female. I went back in his history to see how many times he had made stops after work and saw that it was kind of consistent. Finally, I felt I'd seen enough, and I couldn't hold it in anymore nor wait until he got home, so I called him one night while he was out and told him to stay the hell wherever he was because I was done. He immediately began to panic and tried to state his case. He declared that it wasn't what I thought, and he would explain when he got home. He got home and told me that he had been delivering some narcotics for someone after hours and was getting paid extra money. (Basically Drug dealing) He said he knew that I wouldn't approve, so he didn't tell me about it. He had me look in the drawer near our bed, and there was a box I knew nothing about, and in the box was cash that I knew nothing about. So although I was leery, I believed his story. Well, I believed him but not completely.

I can remember checking his phone after that incident, and I didn't find much of anything of concern, but I can recall that his FB Messenger showed that he'd been communicating with a mutual friend of ours. The messages were erased, but FB Messenger still shows the most recent folks communicated with. I noted it in my mind but didn't overthink it because this particular person was someone who I considered a mutual friend. We will call her "K". "K" had been around since I was about fifteen years old because she was dating the cousin of my very first boyfriend (the father of my child). So she had a kid by the cousin, and I had a kid by him, so we were close at one point in time because our kids were cousins, and we were both working and struggling our way through difficult relationships at that time. Over the years, we lost touch, but Facebook/social media brought us back in contact, and it was like no time had passed. We reconnected via social media, spoke on the phone a couple of times, made plans but never quite got around to hooking up to hang out. Much the same as 75% of all the other longtime long-lost friends of mine on Facebook. Facebook is a way to stay in contact from afar. Anyway, she was a friend of mine, so I knew that it couldn't have been anything shady. They had messaged, but there were no messages to show, so I dismissed it. I looked through the other messages and saw nothing concerning them. A few days later, I checked his smart watch one morning while he was in the shower. Low and behold, I saw text messages from a female I didn't know. It wasn't anything incriminating per se, but it was a female friend programmed under Jennifer's name that I knew nothing about. I didn't immediately bring it up to him because I wanted to gather more info first. Because I knew full well by now that, unless I came with red-handed facts, this man was going to lie to me with no hesitation.

I began to look at his watch each time he left it out, and a couple of days later, he went to work on a Saturday and forgot his watch at home. I immediately went through it again, and I noticed that the Jennifer girl he'd been communicating with was in there a lot more. She referred to running into him recently and how it was good to see him. There were several other good morning and good night messages, and a message, in particular, blew my mind. In one message, she spoke of her, deciding not to keep the baby. I could only read one side of the conversation, but I was out of my mind pissed off, as you can imagine. I felt like my world was shattering again, and everything that I thought was true and real was falling apart again. I just knew that what I was reading couldn't have been correct because he absolutely couldn't be cheating. Nope, I refused to believe it because how could he when I always knew where he was. And what is this about a baby?!?! How could he when he didn't have any free time. All he did was go to work and come home. He never spent any other time outside of with us, his family, so there was no time for him to cheat even if he wanted to. Plus, I know this fool knew full and well that I was not about to put up with that shit again under no circumstances, especially since he'd worked so damn hard to restore our relationship. So as much as he valued our relationship, I couldn't believe or didn't believe he was back cheating.

One thing I did know was there was a whole lot of disrespect going on by entertaining some woman I knew nothing about. By this time, we'd been married for twelve years, so there was no confusion on old or new friends of the opposite sex. There absolutely should not be any communication going on that the other knew nothing about. So this indeed was a violation, and a huge one based on the messages read. The message that spoke about a baby got me the most because I wanted to know what baby she was referring to and when this so-called baby situation happened. I could feel the fire coming out of my pores. I was hot!!! I knew that I was way too upset to confront him in our home because our boys were there, and I didn't want to act a fool in front of them. I could not believe that this jackass had done this shit again. It was unreal. My marriage was over in my heart and mind, and I couldn't wait to confront him. So I waited until it was time for him to be on his way home from work, and then I drove down the street to a school near our house and parked in the lot. I devised a plan to get him to come to where I was by acting like my car was messed up because one good thing about him was that I could always count on him to come running to my rescue. So I called him and told him that my car had a flat and asked him to change my tire. I knew he would come because he had a savior mentality when it came to me. He would cross any ocean, mountain, or sea to get to me if I needed help, so I knew telling him I was in distress would be the key to get him to come where I was. So, of course, he shows up and immediately notices that I have no flat tire, so I ask him to get in my car with me to talk, and he gets in.

As soon as he got in the passenger seat and closed the door, I immediately but calmly asked him, "who is Jennifer?" His expression changed, and it was at this point, he realized that shit was about to get real. He explained to me that Jennifer is nobody but an old friend who he dated in the past and had recently come back in contact with because she had a really bad domestic violence court case going on. He says they saw each other for the first time when she showed up at the courthouse he worked at for her DV case. They exchanged information because she wanted his help with navigating through the court system for her case. He explained that she lived out of state in Oregon and wasn't a threat to me nor a love interest. He also said that he didn't do anything with her; he was trying to be a friend because she had questions about the court process. He admitted that when they dated long before we got married and ended up pregnant, they didn't keep it. When I asked him to prove it and call her right then and there, he obliged and called her phone. She didn't answer, so I asked him to text her to call him, and he did. We sat for a short while, and the whole time I was fuming mad. I asked him to call her again, and she again didn't answer, nor did she call back. At this point, I was ready to see both sides of the conversation at least so that I could determine what was true or not for myself, so I asked him to let me look at his phone. He handed over his phone to me and

I went to his texts and searched through all of the text messages to find that the messages between him and her were erased. This INFURIATED me because this was the ONLY way I felt like I could determine once and for all if what he was saying to me was true by reading and interpreting the messages for myself.

When I saw that the messaged were deleted, my rage was no longer containable. I went smooth off!! I am usually a calm and cool-headed person but baby, let me tell you it felt like the devil himself infiltrated my entire soul. I had never felt that kind of anger before, even when he'd done the past's ultimate betrayal. I was out of control, and my mouth spewed out nothing but venom. I can't even recall all of the words that came out of my mouth or the sentiments expressed, but what I can tell you is that it was the worst tongue lashing he'd ever experienced from me, and it was the closest I'd ever come to being ready to do physical harm to him. I have never been an advocate for violence in a relationship, and that comes from not just men to women but also from women to men. I don't respect anyone who resorts to violence, so it was alarming that I was so angry that I felt very close to it. Once my tirade ultimately ended, I'd clearly expressed to him that our relationship was over and done with. I was not putting up with this bullshit anymore. He tried to reason with me and tried to explain that nothing was going on. He felt like I was overreacting to end our marriage of twelve years over a misunderstanding of messages. I didn't care. I was over it and done. I told him I wanted him out. I felt like even if there wasn't anything sexual going on, he was still out of line for the disrespect of once again entertaining another woman. He knew better, and he knew the consequences, so I didn't care about anything he had to say.

He refused to give up and kept trying to talk to me about it, but I wasn't budging. He then decided to take it to a place that he'd never taken it before. See, he had cried these tears before when we were close to breaking up in the past, so I knew these tears. He had real tears too. These were those tears where you can see the agony in his soul. But those damn tears meant nothing to me this time. Previous times he was able to get me to soften up with his tears and empathize in his sad stories about his childhood traumas being a big part of his dysfunctional behavior. That had worked in the past, with me ultimately feeling empathy for him, and so my heart allowed myself to want to believe him so much that I would allow myself to try again. But not this time!!! Nope, I wasn't budging from the tears. The childhood trauma to feel sorry for him didn't move me, and the agony he was going through caused no change in my decision. I knew that this was the right decision, and I was sticking by it this time, so none of that stuff worked. He had already used those tickets.

Suicidal Thoughts
"Don't Hurt Yourself" - Beyoncé

So what would he pull out of his pocket next? He had exhausted all other avenues of excuses by this time. So this time, he pulled out a suicide threat. He threatened that he didn't want to live without me, and if we were not together, he would take his life. He said that his life has always been messed up from childhood until now. He just was never able to maintain a happy life. He was hurting from a deep place and feeling very sorry for himself and felt like he didn't want to live this life anymore. He expressed his feelings about his life, always being full of despair, and the people he always loved either mistreated him or left him, and he was tired of feeling disappointed. I remember this day clearly because it was one of the scariest days of my life. I was at work, and so was he. He kept calling/texting me to reason with me not to leave him, and when he realized this time was different, he was actually about to lose his marriage and family. I could tell he was unraveling in a different way. He talked about suicide as being the only way he saw out if he would lose his family, and it shook me to my core.

I was terrified and alarmed at his mindset, so I immediately left work on a break and raced to our home to get rid of the gun that belonged to him. I called and had his brother pick it up so that he wouldn't find it in the house. I then went back to work, feeling a little better that the gun was out of the house. The whole drive back to work, I couldn't shake the thoughts of him potentially killing himself. I felt like I'd be partly responsible in some way. I couldn't imagine him not being around anymore to help care for our boys. He wasn't the world's best husband and father, but he was needed and necessary in our lives. Since he was responsible for picking the boys up from school each day because their school was near his job, I was anxiously and nervously waiting to see how this would all play out. By the end of the workday, If he was willing to still pick them up from school, I figured that would mean that he was well enough in his mind to not be thinking about suicide. Usually, I am always first to arrive home from work, so when I came home from work that day, I was planning on waiting to see if he would get our boys from school or not. However, when I got home from work, I saw that he had already picked the boys up early and then dropped them off at our house, but he was nowhere to be found. I asked the boys if he said anything, and they said he was acting weird and told them that he loved them very much, and then he left. I went into our bedroom, and I was in for quite an alarming surprise. I couldn't believe my eyes. It was like a tornado hit.

He always kept his gun at the top of our closet in a box, and I could see that area was a mess. In addition to that, all the dresser drawers were pulled out, and there were papers rambled through, so it was clear that someone was in the room and searching for something specific. I realized at that moment that he had come home early and was searching for the gun. I became frantic because I would be devastated if he killed himself despite everything that went down. I loved him still, of course, despite anything we'd ever gone through or was going through, I didn't want him to die. He was my children's' father, and he was my husband, and after 14years, this was the longest relationship I'd been in for most of my adult life.

Whether he was cheating on me or not, I didn't want anything bad to happen to him. I was horrified that he would contemplate taking his life, and the ransacked room only proved it. So I began to call his phone over and over again. No answer. I kept calling his phone back to back, and he wouldn't answer. I even tried to use the app to see his whereabouts, but nothing showed up because by then, he had turned his phone off. I kept praying and asking God to protect him even from himself. I was so worried and didn't know what to do, so I called up all of his friends & family asking if they'd heard from him. Anybody whose number I had, I called, and nobody had heard from him or seen him. I even tried texting the Jennifer girl to see if she'd heard from him but got no answer or response.

I felt so scared and had so many thoughts running through my head. I kept thinking, what if he kills himself and it's all over a possible misunderstanding? If he didn't sleep with this girl, all of this is over text messages from an ex. I mean, I kinda believed him that nothing more was going on with this Jennifer, especially since she lived in another state.

Regardless, he was still very much out of line and disrespectful even if there was no sex involved. I was truly conflicted because, as done as I was with him and our relationship, I didn't feel like it was worth my husband killing himself. I would blame myself, and I would feel responsible for my boys not having a father. My oldest son's father had already passed away by then, so this would mean that none of my three boys would have a father. I felt like blood would be on my hands, so I had to find him and make sure he didn't hurt himself. I kept calling and calling and leaving messages and got nothing. I thought he might drive his car into a ditch or jump off the bridge since he didn't have the gun.

I was frantic, but all at the same time, I had to hide my worry and feelings from my boys, who knew nothing of what was going on. They had no idea that we were in the midst of one of our marriage's darkest moments. They didn't realize that our family dynamic was about to change permanently, and they had no inkling that they were very close to losing their father. I sat outside the house and cried. I truly didn't know what to do, so I did the last thing that I could think of and the one thing I hated to do and called the police. I remember going to sit outside to wait for the police to come because the boys were in the house, and I didn't want to alert them that something was wrong. The officers came by and took a statement and told me they would put an alert out for his license plate to do a well-check if they noticed him on the road, but there was very little else they could do. I was so hurt & devastated all I could do is sit there and cry once they left. After what seemed like me shedding my entire soul in tears, I got myself together and went back inside the house and cooked dinner and went on as normal as possible for the boys.

I remember sitting in my room that night wondering and thinking if this was how it was supposed to end? It was very hard for me. I reflected on how strongly I believed that there was no way this man would cheat again because he knows better!

So I kept wondering if maybe I shouldn't just end it like this and instead try and find a resolution. I was conflicted because how many times in the past had I gone through this type of shit with him? I'd already promised myself never again, but what do I do when I had no solid proof either way?!

After talking it out with a few confidants, I remained so very confused and conflicted. I no longer knew for sure if I wanted to disrupt our whole life, especially if there was no solid proof of actual cheating. I think at that point. My heart began to soften. I just really wanted things to be okay. Well, I eventually fell asleep that night after constantly praying that he was alive and ok. I woke up in the middle of the night to him, coming into the room very quietly. Upon seeing him, all I could do was hug him. I was very grateful to him being there alive and well, and I knew then that there must still be some life left in our marriage.

He had some explaining to do and proving to do before I could let this thing go. He poured his heart out, trying to convince me that he wasn't cheating. I needed him to prove to me that nothing was going on, and although he was trying and was very convincing, nothing could suffice because those messages were deleted. At this point, it didn't even matter what the girl Jennifer said if we ever got her on the line because she could be saying it to cover. At this point it didn't matter what he said the conversation was about because I only had access to one side. I wanted to see the entire conversation and make my own determination. So at this point, I had to take all the evidence I had and weigh it against what he was telling me, which was an award-winning performance, I might add. Queue, Rihanna's "Take a Bow" -*How about a round of applause? A standing ovation you put on quite a show really had me goin'*. In the end, I couldn't see myself walking away from twelve years (fourteen if you include the years before we got married) over just the "possibility" that something happened. We had a family, our boys were getting older, and one of the last things I ever wanted to do is raise my little black boys as a single parent because I knew life would be harder on them without having a dad in the house. So I had to choose, and of the two roads ahead, I decided to stay given that I didn't have any real solid proof of actual sex, leaving room for me to be willfully ignorant.

On that suicidal night that he came home, and we hugged, then talked it out. We also cried together and poured his heart out about how he felt like his life was cursed. He had been through so much as a little boy. He's always been searching for the love that his parents & grandparents fumbled early in his life. I didn't realize it until we talked that night just how much this created an emptiness inside him, a sort of brokenness and void within.

I realized at this point that this void was something that he had tried relentlessly to fix within himself in all the wrong ways. He did this by seeking the attention/love/sex/affection etc... from women. It was a deeper issue. But the reality is that none of those things would ever be able to fix that problem. It would only temporarily quench the symptoms.

That night when he told me how he felt, I also told him in all honesty how I truly felt. It was like I had woken up and realized for the first time what we both truly needed. It was one of the hardest things to say and admit, but I told him the truth: I didn't believe that we were supposed to be together. I didn't believe that I was the right person for him. I didn't feel like I was his soul mate. As hard as it was to say and admit, I felt very strongly that it was true. It was a realization that I'd come to, long before then but ignored because I didn't want to accept that the father of my kids was not the man I was supposed to be with. I didn't want to acknowledge that I didn't feel like he was my soul mate. I knew it deep inside, but it was validated in my heart at that moment that night.

I struggled with love, with being in love or feeling in love throughout our relationship. I didn't know or understand my feelings and why they would be fleeting and dismissive at times. I wasn't sure what type of love I had, but I didn't feel like it was the kind of love that a wife needed to have for her husband. That night, and at that moment, I felt a different and deeper kind of real love for him. I looked at the man before me, and I saw what he needed to be whole, and I knew it wasn't me. I thought back to the 2007 incident years earlier when I told him I'd never be able to love or respect him again fully, and although I knew then I wasn't lying, I could see the proof now in how our relationship had progressed. No matter how much I loved him, or he loved me, I knew that we were not meant to be. Yet, I stayed.

One of the things that the incident in 2016 taught me or forced me to acknowledge was that our relationship was hollow. Yea, it looked pretty on the outside, and yea, it had stood the test of time and outlasted many other relationships. Still, it wasn't the happy, loving relationship that it appeared to be on the outside and on social media. It was very rare being a black two-parent household amongst those around us, so a lot of other people looked up to us and the longevity that we were able to accomplish within our relationship. That too weighed heavily on me.

Two Years Later
"Forever Don't Last" - *Jazmine Sullivan*

The next two years or so were probably thee most unproblematic years of our entire marriage. We ended up seeing another counselor for a short time, an older black man in Hayward who was a behaviorist. He was very different from all the rest of the counselors we'd gone to in the past. He gave us some great advice, and we began to improve on all cylinders. Our boys were getting bigger, and we were operating as a family unit should. There were no incidents of concern. I didn't feel like he was up to no good. We were getting along for the longest consistent time ever. In the past, we would always seem to get into arguments right before special events or dates. For instance, one year, we got into a really bad argument before Valentine's Day, another year. It was before our anniversary. It became so common that we no longer even spent much effort in celebrating special days. The most we would do is maybe go to dinner for our anniversary. But besides that, our relationship was pretty smooth sailing for the last few years. His whereabouts were never questioned. He spent all his free time at home and all the other time at work. I started to have some hope that maybe our relationship was supposed to be, maybe I was unrealistic in my thoughts or hopes of a marriage that invoked inner feelings and emotions of deep true love & happiness. We weren't living that fairytale love, but we were the happiest we'd been in a long time.

I couldn't even recall the last time I was pissed at him to a level of pisstivity, which used to happen quite often. In the past, when I got pissed at him, the first thing out of my mouth was usually - I'm DONE. I was ready to end our relationship every time he pissed me off. I almost sort of used it as a weapon after a while because I knew it would get him to do whatever I pretty much wanted. If we disagreed about anything, the moment I'd get pissed, it was as if all my feelings left my heart. I could and would stop talking to him for daysssss and sometimes weeks at a time. When I wasn't pleased, it was no longer a happy home. I created a toxic environment that he hated anytime we got into it. I would withhold sex because I knew there was nothing he'd like more than sex, so until I got what I wanted, that was out. None of this makes me proud. I realize now how stupid and immature my actions were.

I realize now there were a lot of mistakes I too made within our marriage. The first mistake was saying I do... ha-ha... no, no, take that back. He and I getting married was a part of the plan for my life, which helped shape me into the woman I've grown to be today. So I can never really say I regret it. The only thing I sort of regret is not leaving the relationship sooner because I had a very good reason several times, but I have to believe that also was all a part of a bigger plan.

So obviously, the relationship ended at some point, which is why this book even exists. Let's go ahead and finally explore what straw finally broke this camel's back. Saturday morning, October 6th of 2018, changed everything for me. It began the night before when I was in bed, scrolling through the internet after returning home late from a bartending gig. My hubby was at work as he always is on Saturday nights as a bouncer. Things had been really good, so I was feeling kind of frisky. I decided that maybe I'll wait up for him and give him some. At about 1:30 am, he messaged me on Facebook and asked me what I was still doing up? I guess he saw my green light on which indicates that I was actively online. I was confused about why he was messaging me on Facebook instead of texting or calling me, that was quite strange, but I shook it off and just responded. I told him I wasn't sleepy once I got home from work.

He began to chit chat with me on messenger, explaining how he was bored at work and how he wanted to come home to me early. I told him to see if they would let him leave, and he said he'd try. This whole exchange was weird because we never usually chatted via messenger, and he also never asked about leaving early. After that message, Instead of staying up and waiting for him, I went to sleep.

I didn't know that I'd fallen asleep for the last time as the pseudo-semi-happily married woman I was. That next morning I had plans to go hiking with my sisters-in-law. My husband's sisters and I were all meetings up early to hike, so I had to wake up early, but my husband had gotten up even earlier than me because he had to go work as a ref at an early football game. I awakened that morning to him just standing over me, staring at me. I could feel him standing over me and not saying anything. I pretended to be asleep and kept my eyes closed, but I was confused. I thought to myself, why is he just standing and staring at me and not saying anything? When he never moved, I decided to open my eyes to alert him that I was aware of his presence over me. He then seemed to snap out of it and leaned over to kiss me goodbye and told me he loves me. In my mind, I was thinking he's acting weird, but whatever.

He left for work, and I eventually got up and got ready to make it to my sister-in-law's house on time. On the way out my oldest son asked for a ride to Bart to visit with his girlfriend, so I agreed to drop him off on the way, and we both ran out to the car and jumped inside. Once we jumped inside, I realized that I had been so busy rushing to get ready that morning that I hadn't even checked my phone yet for messages/texts or anything else. I finally looked at my phone and saw a message to me on Facebook from an old friend of mine. The message was from our friend, "K".

The message read as follows: "I have been seeing your husband off and on for two years. My son's father saw the messages and told me to tell you, so I did." I hadn't even pulled out of my driveway yet when I read this message. I was confused and almost amused because I knew there was NO WAY this could say what I thought it was saying. No way. So I pulled off and headed on my way. I couldn't resist picking my phone up and rereading it as I drove towards the freeway, and the look on my face must have alarmed my son because he asked me if I was alright. I was borderline in shock because by now, I had read the message over and over and over again and realized it was saying the unthinkable. My son was concerned, and I couldn't even form the words, so I just handed my phone to him to read the message.

In hindsight, it probably wasn't the best idea to show the message to my son, but my son and I are very close, and he's of age (21 years old), so I kinda just felt like I needed support, and he was there and could help me make sense of things. He was floored and just as disappointed as me. So I finally dropped him off and proceeded on to my sis in laws' house. Once I arrived there, my sister greeted me in her usual bubbly personality, showing me lots of love and explaining how everyone is running behind. I could not hear anything she was saying. I was too numb and totally in shock, so all I could do was put my phone to her face and show her the message. Once she read the message, she too was confused and in shock. Eventually, my other sisters-in-law arrived, and we all began to sit around and try to dissect this situation and what was going on. I was on edge because I felt like on one hand, this message had to be some joke or mistake because there is no possible way he and she would do some shit like this to me. Nope, I refused to believe that. But on the other hand, thinking about the past and who he used to be seven or eight years ago, I knew he had it in him to cheat and be disrespectful. I just didn't think he would be that damn stupid ever again.

Immediately I began to think back to a few years earlier. Remember when I had those feelings and went through his phone, and saw recent messages from "K", "our" mutual friend? Well, that all came rushing back to my memory as I was trying to dissect and make sense of this message I just received from her. It was so unbelievable to me initially that I laughed it off. My message back to her was so lighthearted because I did not believe her or this. So I kept trying to message her back and even tried calling her because yes, I had her phone number in my phone since forever because we were old friends. Unfortunately, she wouldn't respond to any of the messages, and the number I had for her was an old one and no longer worked. I tried reaching out to a mutual friend of ours who also happens to be her best friend, so I knew she had her number, but she refused to give me her number, stating that she didn't give out other people's phone numbers. This response threw me for a loop because this was someone who I had hung out extensively with. We all three used to hang out together, so she knew I wasn't just anyone off the street asking for her number. I was perplexed that she didn't want to give me her number, and then it dawned on me that she must have known about it. Since I couldn't get through to her, I switched gears and tried reaching out to "K's" son's father, whom she claimed was the whistleblower in her original message. I'd known him for years since I was about fifteen years old. I'd met "K" through him because he was the cousin of my oldest son's father. Our kids were cousins. So yes, I felt comfortable contacting him directly as the source.

Well long story short, after several texts and FB messages, he finally responded and told me he was at work but would call me back as soon as he gets off at 7 pm. Me and my sis-in-laws spent the whole rest of the day drinking tequila and talking this whole thing through. My best friend Jenise even came over for extra support and we all just kind of tried to make sense of this. I had no appetite at all, so I never touched a bite of food, and despite drinking shots of tequila all day, I somehow didn't feel the effects of it at all. I must have been too pissed to be impacted by the liquor. Who knew that it was possible to be too mad to get drunk?

I was so eager for time to pass so that I could get that call. In the meantime, my husband sent me a text asking me if I wanted to accompany him to a party or hang out with him? I knew he was only texting me to see if he could gauge if I were angry or not. By now, I knew that he was aware that this girl had messaged me and spilled the beans. I figured that's why he had messaged me the night before, and that was why he was standing over me just staring at me that morning. He knew that I was going to hear from her that day. So rather than letting him know what I knew, I kept it simple and just told him no. He was inviting me to attend a party that initially he planned to attend alone, so I knew that he was trying to fish. Finally, after several hours of tequila and angst, it was 7 pm. I was sitting in extreme anticipation, waiting for this call. The whole time I am thinking, this phone call would finally confirm what was going on. This phone call was going to be the single determining factor behind if my marriage was once and for all over or not. 7:01 and nothing… 7:02 nothing, and by now, I am ready to explode!!! I had to talk myself into giving him at least five minutes of a grace period. I assumed he had to get in his car or leave the building or something. At 7:05, I couldn't take it anymore, and I texted him to see if he was still going to call. Finally, a few moments later, he called.

The Call That Ended It All
"In the Air" - Teyana Taylor

In that phone call, I learned the fate of my marriage. I learned that life as I'd previously known it was over for good. In the call, he explained that he was over his son's mom's house to have sex with her because that was their arrangement. He would come and go as he pleased. While at her home this time, they both got really drunk and began going through each other's phones as a joke. Well, when he went through her phone, he noticed messages between her, and my husband and they were the wrong kind of messages to and from a married man. So he confronted her about it, and she admitted to him what had been going on. He was so disgusted with how trifling she had stooped. Especially since she was the pursuer, he had known me since I was that young, naive fifteen-year-old girl who dated his cousin. We were family at this point, which was why he felt compelled to let me know what was going on. So he told her that she needed to tell me, or he would tell me himself, which prompted her to send me that message.

After that, I can remember driving home in a fog and going into the house in a daze. When I finally made it home and walked into our bedroom, my husband was in there getting dressed after showering. He was getting ready to attend the party he asked me about earlier. The nerve of this fool to still try and attend a party knowing full well that his marriage was in jeopardy. He began to try his hand at some small talk, but I wasn't responding to anything he said to me, and every time he tried to talk small talk to me, it only made me angrier and angrier. So finally, I just blurted out, are you going to stand there and act like nothing is going on? At first, he tried to play dumb and ask what? But I guess the look on my face prompted him to cut the shit, and he immediately began to apologize and try to explain. The words he spoke meant nothing. Like literally, nothing he said meant anything at all to me. I could barely even hear him from the noise of my thoughts. I can recall him saying something about it wasn't that serious. She pursued him and he got weak because he didn't expect it and was pressured. Saying things like she was nothing but an easy lay. He loves me. She wanted him to leave me, but he refused. He ended it a long time ago. He loves me. He's sorry. It was two years ago. He stopped it. Blah blah blah blah blah! It all sounded like someone using their nails to scratch the chalkboard to me.

All that I knew at this moment was that it was indeed over. This time was different, and I felt it deep in my soul. I was done in a way that I'd never felt before. Yes, this time was indeed different. I wasn't even really mad. I wasn't really sad. I couldn't "feel" anything at all. But I knew that our relationship had reached the point of no return and what solidified it is the peace that I felt inside. I felt like this decision, as hard as it was, was the only decision available. I was done dealing with this broken man in this broken relationship and over these broken vows. I was done, and I was surprisingly at peace. A peace that I can't even really explain, but somehow I knew that God was releasing me from this relationship, and I found peace and solace in that.

In the days and weeks that followed, he tried his damndest to change my mind. He tried every single thing he could think of, including another suicide threat. But I wasn't affected by anything he said or came up with. I was at peace with my decision, and I wasn't going to change my mind. He had been given ample time to get his shit together. I guess you can say some awakening happened. It was as if I finally had an epiphany about the reality of my situation. Deep down in my soul, I knew that I would be not just okay, but more than okay. I didn't know how I would pay the bills by myself, especially since we had just recently moved to a more expensive place, but I didn't worry or care about it. I felt very strongly that God would take care of me, and I would be okay. There were no doubts that my boys and I would be okay, so I left all fears in the rearview and my broken marriage.

Over the next few days, weeks, and months, I learned a lot about myself and what love is and isn't. I knew that I hadn't fully loved or given my all to him or our marriage, contributing to several of our problems and issues. None of which excuses the many infidelities and the disrespect that happened. I was able to reconcile and forgive myself for my part and completely move on. We were married for just under fourteen years at this point, and after the end of any relationship, there is a grieving process that is normal and expected. I believe I went through my grieving process in exactly eight days before I had my epiphany moment. I remember being sad, crying, and feeling a huge loss on those days. But, from that eighth day on, not another tear was shed over my "loss" instead, I was in a place of hopeful optimism. I knew that the days ahead were going to be much better than the days behind me. I knew that I deserved better and that I would finally be able to pursue the true love & happiness I yearned for.

I remember stumbling upon a page of someone named April Mason, and she empowers women to value themselves, embrace their femininity, and not settle. One of the things she said, which resonated with me, is that healing is a choice. You get to decide when and how long you want to "feel" and "heal", and I decided that I was done right then. It is funny that many folks will probably say I am crazy for believing that I am healed because I've "decided" to be. Still, I gotta tell you that it is almost two years later in writing this book, and I haven't felt anything less than fully healed and fulfilled in my life ever since. The way to determine if you have healed from a situation or not is to test how talking about it or thinking about it makes you feel. If you still get upset, angry, or feel the need to hash it out or prove a point. You very likely aren't healed yet. Let's say you have a cut on your arm when it is unhealed, every time you touch it, it still hurts. But once it heals, you can touch it and rub it all you want and not feel that immense pain it caused before. It may still hurt, but it will be minimal, and it may leave a scar (a reminder), but that cut has healed.

In the months to follow, I experienced and developed "The Escape Plan" for leaving toxic relationships or any relationships that no longer serve you. The escape plan is a series of honest truths and a blueprint I learned, experienced, and utilized as the footstool for my strength and confirmation that I needed to escape my toxic relationship. We will revisit this escape plan later in the book.

Bittersweet Lessons

Part 2

The Lessons

Bittersweet Lessons

Lesson 1

Don't Ignore Red Flags

After all of the previous failed relationships of mine, I can honestly say that one lesson became very clear in hindsight. This very first lesson of importance is do NOT ignore red flags!

Man, oh man, how I wish someone had pulled me to the side and gave me this very serious and crucial bit of advice. It may have saved me a lot of heartaches had I received it from a credible source. The main purpose of this book is to impart the things to you that I wish someone would have shared with me. So if you don't take anything else from this reading, please take this particular lesson to heart. Red flags are the signs that you and that person are not compatible, and ignoring them is a mistake.

We were all given something very special inside of us called intuition. I believe that we ladies were given a double dose. This special double dose of intuition is there for a reason. It speaks to us when things are not quite right. When red flags occur, our intuition will almost always begin to whisper to us to take heed. The problem is that we tend to cover up that intuition with justifications and excuses to keep indulging. Well, I am here to tell you what we both know you already know: you should always trust your gut!! We are equipped with this valuable tool to keep us out of danger, and you can best believe a relationship can be a danger to your heart, spirit, and life if it is the wrong one.

Ladies, when we get into our new relationships, you know how we are and how we act. We are pretty hard to talk to when it comes to our shiny brand-new man. He is everything plus some in our eyes, thanks to those rose-colored glasses we usually have on. You know how it is when you like this new guy, and you're hopeful for what's to come. In some instances, you've already started imagining your future life together with the house, the kids, the dog, and yes, even the white picket fence. It's best that we not even lie to ourselves because we know that once we get so engrossed in the possibilities, we let our guard down and let things slide. Next thing you know, we suddenly start giving the benefit of the doubt when we know we shouldn't. We have all been here before, I am sure. This is typically normal behavior, typical... yes. But is it healthy? No! Do you know what we are doing when we ignore red flags? We are trying to avoid disappointment. Denial feels a lot better than the truth when the truth hurts.

So what happens next? We start seeing these things or behaviors that we don't like. We start hearing that voice inside, asking us what in the hell are you doing? We start feeling that lump of intuition within our spirit, and what do we typically do in these moments? Once we hear that internal alarm goes off, we typically begin to talk ourselves into believing it's a false alarm. We start second-guessing the facts, and we start to downplay the warning signs. During this time, it is likely that an internal struggle is going on. The mind is telling you one thing, but your heart is changing it into another. Flag after flag we see, and we see them clearly, but we begin to justify their actions with excuses. Why do we do this? I'll say it again. Denial feels a lot better than the truth when the truth hurts.

Here's a question you should ask yourself. Can you truly be completely happy with someone who does "insert red flag"? I mean, think about it. If whatever that issue is, is a problem for you, why are you even contemplating? What is there to mull over? You know there are certain standards that you've set for yourself and your relationships. When those standards aren't being met, there's nothing to contemplate. Now, of course, I am not saying that you become cutthroat about your desires to the point where you are cutting people off without giving them a fair shot. But, you and I both know that certain things are non-negotiables. Sometimes it isn't so much about the red flag's act and what the act is saying about the person's real character. That is what you should always focus on is the person's character. Your non-negotiables are likely different from mine... mine are different from hers, and hers are different than ours, but we all have our expectations and limits, and we all set certain standards that must be met. The problem isn't having standards; the problem is when we don't uphold them.

There are many behaviors that Mr. or Mrs. Wrong will exhibit, which will surely ring that inner alarm to alert you of a red flag. He or she could be super sweet and charming and then show signs that they're manipulative. They may do all the things you like initially, and then you notice after while most of it tapers off. They might even still give you lots of love and affection, but it comes at the expense of wanting to control you and the relationship. The red flags often start as little things. Things that trigger the alarm but don't quite set it off. Those little things are significant and should be analyzed accordingly. I would advise you to pay close attention to those things and be honest with yourself about what the underlying meaning is to those particular actions. For example, if the guy you are dating doesn't have any respect for his mother or talks bad to and about his mother or children's mother, would that not set off a red flag? If you pay close attention, it shows that he has the propensity also to disrespect you without a second thought. If your mate is showing slight signs of behavioral concerns now in the very beginning, what makes you think that over time, that behavior will not progress? You see, most people present their "representative" in the early stages of the relationship. This means that they are their absolute best selves and on their best behavior. The signs you can catch in this early stage are especially important to be taken seriously because if they are working to be on their best behavior and something of concern rears itself, it means that their real character is bursting through that "representative." You are getting a glimpse into something that they were probably trying to keep under wraps, so imagine once more time goes by, and this person now feels comfortable enough to drop the act?

I want you to think about some of your past relationships for a second or maybe even your current relationship. I want you to be honest with yourself and think about any red flags you saw or noticed but talked yourself out of leaving the relationship. I know that it's happened to you before because it's happened to us all. I think about my previous relationships, and I can name three red flags off top that I noticed in three of my relationships that I ignored or justified somehow.

In my very first relationship, first and foremost, **Red Flag #1**, he was controlling. He wanted me to act how he wanted me to act; he wanted me to listen to him like I was his child, and that didn't work for me. I've never been one who did well with folks telling me what to do.

Red Flag #2, he was heavily influenced by the streets. I knew of illegal activities such as drugs, guns, stolen cars, and robberies, and I knew I was not about that life at all. Although I grew up in the hood, I was an onlooker rather than a participant. A square is what they call that. I knew that my square ass would never be satisfied & happy in a relationship with a man who straddled both sides of the law. No, sir, not me.

Red Flag #3, he had very unrealistic views on what a woman should do/be to her man. He wanted me to worship the ground he walked on and throw all caution to the wind for him. He wanted me to love him more than I loved myself, and that was never going to happen because although I may have struggled with love, I always loved myself enough to not put anybody before myself. Not until I had my son.

So although he would talk down to me so bad that I would sometimes question myself, I always loved myself. It's funny because, in the beginning, I saw these signs, and I recognized the red flags even at fifteen years old. But despite seeing those red flags, I wanted the fairytale to be real so bad that I pushed them to the side. Well, look where that got me? Pregnant at seventeen years old, miserable, and afraid for my life. Lesson learned.

In my next long-term relationship, I recognized several red flags as well.

Red flag #1. He was way too old for me; the man was nine years older than me when I met him at nineteen years old. They say that age ain't nothing but a number, but I would have to say that looking back, I wouldn't recommend becoming involved with such an older man while I was so young. Although I was a very independent and mature nineteen-year-old from having a kid early, I still had too much growing to do. I couldn't even legally drink alcohol, and here I am pursuing a relationship with a grown man.

Red Flag #2. He wasn't very affectionate at all nor fun. What I mean by that is I noticed early on that the affection and feelings he displayed initially at the beginning of our relationship did not continue. He was quite attentive and showed his deep feelings for me, but that all disappeared once we passed the honeymoon stage. He also didn't like to do very much outside of the house, and I wanted somebody who wanted to get out and see the world. He was happy with staying put, eating a nice steak on the couch while watching tv. But I wanted to do something fun rather than the same thing all the time. That drained a lot of the life from this relationship.

Last but not least, **Red Flag #3.** He was just too damn cheap/frugal for me. Now I can understand and even appreciate a man that is responsible with his spending. He was very responsible and had great credit to show for it. But the thing that I can't get with is when I feel like it's pulling teeth to get you to spend money or pay bills. He had no problem with paying half on most of the bills, but he would always be sure not to do no more, no less. Initially, upon moving in, he never even offered help on the bills. I had to ask him to contribute. If that's not a red flag, I don't know what is.

Another example is that he was always hesitant about going out and spending money on dinner or dates, but I will say that he would finally flip the switch and go all out when it came to birthdays or Christmas. These are behaviors that I recognized early enough in the relationship that I could have taken into account and gotten out. I would have saved myself two years had I taken heed to those red flags because I knew the relationship wasn't sustainable. Those red flags showed that we had different views and priorities, and it was other things that made us happy.

Relationship #3. Where do I even begin? Oh, I guess I can start with **Red Flag #1**. He was a damn liar. From the onset of our relationship, this man lied about so many different things that it was alarming. They were mostly little white lies or an exaggeration of sorts such as lying about his job title, lying about attending church (and paying tithes), and moved up to lying about how many children he had in a roundabout way. Those little lies were red flags that I should've taken more seriously because those little lies turned into a relationship full of lies of all sizes, shapes, and forms.

Red Flag #2. He was a cheater. Once I caught him cheating in the early stages of our relationship, and he responded that "we never made it official" I should have known. I mean, really, dude?!? I know it's only been a few months, but we had talked of marriage already, which, in my opinion, shows a clear intent on making this a serious relationship. Oh, and oh yeah, the fact that I was PREGNANT, and he had that mindset should have shown me who I was dealing with. It was bad enough he didn't even meet the criteria for all my standards, but add the lies and cheating in and the red flags in my face gave me every reason to walk away from this relationship.

Lastly, **Red Flag #3** He wasn't a very good father, and I also saw that early on. The fact that he was pretty much okay with being a deadbeat in his children's lives and that he justified those actions was a clear sign of a mindset about parenting that I was not on board with. Unfortunately, this mindset eventually reared its head throughout our relationship once we had our kids and then bit me in the ass again once our marriage ended. He once again showed his lack of priority for being a parent.

With everything I know now about red flags, I would have taken different steps in some, if not all, of my previous relationships. How I wish someone would have pulled my coattail with this info and provided me with the steps that would help me back then. But hopefully, that's where this book comes in for you or someone who needs it. If you recognize any of the signs or red flags you've been ignoring, here is your opportunity to think it through. As you already know, we make certain decisions and choices, which changes the trajectory of our lives and how our life progresses. So if you are trying to avoid stressful, bad, or toxic relationships in your life, the first thing to do is make a choice not to ignore red flags.

There are a few steps that you can take when you encounter concerns or red flags that can help you assess whether or not it is a deal-breaker or not.

Step 1. Set clear standards.
First and foremost, you have to make sure you are clear on your standards from the gate. You have to know without a doubt what you will and will not accept and then stand firm in that. This way, once you notice something that doesn't meet a standard that you have, or causes you to question, you can properly assess if it is a deal-breaker or not.

Step 2. Free your heart & mind.
It's very important that you have healed from any past relationships before you get into new ones. You want to ensure that you are not projecting or bringing anything from your previous relationships into your new relationships. You don't want to suffer from not being able to detect and properly manage any triggers. If not, you will view things from the lenses of your unhealed inner hurt and pain instead of real logic. So step two is about assessing the red flag from a healthy place both mentally and emotionally, and that requires a free heart and mind.

Lastly, Step 3. Love yourself, Enough!
You have to make sure that you are always fully loving yourself. You have got to love yourself enough to not settle for anything less than you deserve. Period. There is never a good reason to settle for less than you are worth, and you won't know that worth unless you begin to love yourself enough. This means getting to know you, the real you. Get comfortable with yourself, with spending time with yourself alone. Get comfortable with pampering yourself and taking care of yourself emotionally, spiritually, and mentally. Make sure your cup overflows with the amount of love and admiration you have for yourself so that you can easily recognize when someone else is not loving you enough. You treat others how to love you by how you love yourself!

So In the end, the main lesson here is that the red flags that you ignore today don't go away. Red flags will lead to red lights you encounter throughout the relationship. Sooner or later, those flags turn into stumbles, which turn into your relationship's eventual train wreck. Ignoring red flags because you want to see the good in a person is like pushing snooze on your internal alarm; you may have quieted your concerns temporarily but give it some time, and that loud, obnoxious ringing is surely to give your behind a startling wakeup call. Do NOT ignore red flags!!

Lesson 2

Trust is Earned

Listen, we all know if there is one thing a relationship requires to stand the test of time; it is trust. To love freely and fully, you must trust. You have to trust that the person you are opening your heart to is going to take care of it. You have to trust that being vulnerable with this person is okay. One of the most freeing feelings in the world is to have complete trust. It is like the sun to flowers; it is what allows the relationship to grow. Trust gives you a sense of security that will translate into confidence and strength.

Whenever you are in a relationship and the trust is broken, you will most certainly be faced with an uphill battle. Sometimes the battle to regain trust is a success, but unfortunately, a lot of times, it is not. There is usually always a little voice of doubt in the back of your mind once trust is broken. Being able to trust your partner is a must! It is much easier to maintain trust than to try and get trust back once it is broken.

Just think about it for a few seconds. Think about when you've been in relationships in the past (or currently) where the trust has been broken. Once you experience that betrayal, it forever impacts how you see that person no matter how much time passes or if you have forgiven them or not. You lose a little bit of respect for a person that you cannot trust. How do I know? Because I am speaking from experience. Let me ask you this, have you ever in your life had a person regain respect back after they've done something detrimental to lose it? Just think about it, has anyone you lost respect for, ever been successful at regaining that same level of respect back? Sure, you may be able to forgive them and even stick around with them, but can you honestly say that you respect & trust them the same? I believe that the answer is no. It is almost impossible to gain trust or respect back, so the reality of the situation is if the trust is an issue, the relationship is already doomed and set to expire. With no trust (or respect), the relationship now has an expiration date. You are once again, only prolonging the inevitable or, like I said before, pressing snooze on the outcome.

The trust in my marriage was demolished very early on. But me being young and a bit naive, I was a believer that people changed and wanted to give him another chance. I didn't yet see it as a sign of a deep character flaw. I wanted to believe him so badly that I allowed myself to learn to trust him again. I can't say that I regained all of the trust, but I was 95% there in my naivety. So, when he betrayed my trust throughout our marriage, I would justify and talk myself into trusting him somehow. After a while, I feel like I truly did gain back the trust. It took a lot of work, and he had to do a lot to prove I could trust him again. After he was caught, those next seven years of our marriage, he did a complete 180 and showed and proved to me that he loved me and didn't want to do anything to jeopardize what he had. This is what I believed I saw so that I could regain the trust back, but respect is something different. I never really regained my respect for him. I can't explain it. I guess deep down inside, I knew that he wasn't worthy of it.

So here's what I will say about trust. You must have smart trust, not blind trust. This means that you need to trust your partner because his or her actions match his or her words, and everything that he or she does and shows you. Not everybody who wants to be trusted can or should be trusted. My ex himself totally and completely believed himself when he vowed never to betray our relationship again. He had no doubts in himself at the time that he made that determination and still failed. So that goes to show you that there are even instances where the person can't even trust themselves. I blindly trusted this man from the onset of our relationship, and unbeknownst to me, he was lying from day one. I trusted him when I saw the big, huge cautionary signs saying stop and the many red flags. I did not have smart trust. I had naive trust and willfully ignorant trust, and I look back now and can realize that. Thankfully, I grew through that and learned quite a few lessons.

As I've mentioned, the reason I wanted to write this book is that I want to share what I know now so that I can hopefully help someone else who may be dealing with something similar. The main lesson that I've learned about trust is that trust must be earned and not given freely. If you don't trust your partner, it's likely for an excellent reason, so if nothing else, trust your gut!!

Bittersweet Lessons

Lesson 3

Let Go Of The Fear

Why do we stay in relationships that no longer serve us? Fear. Man, oh man, it can be sooooo tough to let go and leave a bad or toxic relationship that we have become accustomed to. Why is that? Why do we stay in toxic or unhealthy relationships long past their expiration dates? Is it love? Convenience? Do we believe that eventually, things will change? I believe there are several reasons why a woman probably stays in an unhealthy relationship, but one of the notable reasons is being afraid. Fear of the unknown, of starting over, of the possible consequences, of judgment, how it impacts your children or fear of failure. And then when we finally get the courage or strength to leave, we often end up accepting them right back into our lives after they've lured us back in with empty promises. Why is that? Perhaps fear of being alone.

It is completely normal to have a natural desire to have a mate or partner. Having someone to walk through life with you, face challenges, and love and be loved by is something we all most naturally want. It is not just something we want. It is something we crave. God did not intend for us to be alone; he knew we needed help. Naturally, we find it hard to let a relationship go because we let go of that partnership, that comfort, and love. It's tough to let go of something you crave and need, especially when you do not have anything to replace it with. This is why many rebound relationships occur because the person is trying to hurry up and replace what they fear they are letting go of, which is love & companionship. Fear is normal, but you have to get over your fear because it is only keeping you from something greater. Remember, fear is only "False Evidence Appearing Real,"... so don't let it keep you from getting and having more.

So we understand that fear is normal and also very understandable. I know how hard it is to step out on faith and make decisions when you are not sure where they may lead. It isn't easy to make choices that put you in a situation where you don't know if you will make it. It is also hard to make a sacrifice that may cause a lot of hurt & pain for you or others even when you know that the sacrifice will benefit you later.

Honesty Moment

I want you to be honest with yourself and think back on relationships that you stayed in too long and think about the real reason(s) why you didn't leave sooner, and what the core of that reason was? I can almost bet you that it involved some fear. Fear clouds the truth and paralyzes you into staying put.

As a mother, I know that one of those fears for a mom can negatively impact your children. You are in fear of what it will do to them if you disrupt their lives by leaving the relationship. I know this to be true because I had those same thoughts and fears at one time. Well, let me tell you now. The kids will be okay! Children are resilient, and they benefit far more from being exposed to a loving &

caring environment, whether it is with or without both parents. Exposing children to negative relationships or toxic or dysfunctional relationships will do far more harm than removing children from a two-parent home.

As a mother, one of the things that we inevitably always do is put our children's needs before our own. Your children are the most precious things in the world to you, and you will protect them at all costs, even at your own expense. They always come first. This is how it is, and this is how it should be. However, there is a bit of a caveat in that sentiment. As women, we often overlook that to care for others fully; we have to first take care of ourselves. To build up others, we must build up ourselves. To pour into others, we must first pour into ourselves. This means that if you are in a situation or relationship that does not serve you, you cannot say that you are adequately caring for yourself. Your happiness is just as important as everyone else's, and if you aren't happy, it shows no matter how hard we as mommies try to hide it. I can honestly say that I know and understand first-hand how hard it is to leave a relationship with your children's father because you are feeling inside like the children will suffer. Any action that causes your children to suffer will, of course, cause you to halt or hesitate to take that action. But what I want the mama bears to understand is that you are doing yourself and your children a disservice by exposing them to toxicity and prolonging the inevitable. If your relationship is toxic, it is causing your children to suffer whether you see signs of it now or not. Your children need to be in an environment that is safe, not just physically but also mentally and emotionally. They see, hear, and sense when the relationship is not right or when the relationship is full of drama. They may not show or say anything (or maybe they will), but staying is far worse than temporarily disrupting their lives for a permanent positive change.

If you are using the kids to justify holding on to a broken relationship until the end of time, I'd advise you to think about for a moment if this is something you'd want your child to do? Would you advise your child to stay in a situation that doesn't make them happy, doesn't give them the respect, honor, or joy they deserve? Would you advise your child that a little bit of happiness here and there is acceptable? Would you advise your child that they aren't worth having everything their heart dreams of? Would you advise your child that they should settle with what they can get? If the answer is no, why would you live out those examples in front of their very eyes? You have to be able to practice what you preach. Studies show that it is far more harmful to expose children to negative or toxic relationships than it ever could to leave a bad relationship behind. So take solace in knowing full-heartedly that the children absolutely will be okay when it is time to take care of you! They benefit the most when you are happy and at your best!

Listen, I get it. I know exactly how it feels to want to hang on with the hopes that things will change. You fear that you may be letting go prematurely. Yes, I've been there. But the reality is that once a relationship has certain issues, it is very unlikely you will ever make it back to the place you desire for it.

It's almost like chasing the first high off of a drug; no matter how many times you take a hit, it will never reach the same level nor impact your system on the level it did for the first time. Or are you afraid of starting over or of the unknown? Well, let's think realistically about it. If you step out of your fear and into the possibilities, yes, there is a chance that you will encounter more disappointments or potential heartache along the way. But the thing to remember is that you miss 100% of all the shots you don't take. Meaning, there is also a chance that you are putting yourself in a position for something better, something greater, a blessing that you will miss out on if you don't take that chance. I don't know about you, but I would rather take a shot and miss, even if it's several times if it means that I am going after something I truly want or desire. Eventually, that shot will hit nothing but net!! But you can't receive what God has for you if your hand is too busy grasping onto something you have to let go of first. Look at starting over as a blessing. Someone once said, "Don't be afraid to start over again. This time, you're not starting from scratch, you're starting from experience!"

Fear is a part of life, and we all experience it at several points. When you are making decisions based solely on fear, they more than likely aren't going to be the best decision. You are making a decision based around what "feels" the least problematic. You have to learn that fear isn't bigger than faith. If you don't remember anything else, I want you to remember one thing about fear; everything your heart desires, including freedom, growth, success, and happiness, are ALL on the other side of fear. Let me say that again, everything that you want and everything you desire is on the other side of fear; you have to go and get it. Once you are ready to stand up for your happiness, it requires you to set fear aside. Don't be afraid... walk into your destiny.

Lesson 4

<center>~~~~~~~~~~ ~~~~~~~~~~</center>

Seek God

Matthew 6:33 says: "Seek ye first the kingdom of God, and his righteousness; and all these things shall be added unto you." One of the biggest and most important things to remember when going through a tumultuous situation or, as in this case, a relationship, is that God is here for you. God is the source of your strength and comfort when you need him, but you must seek him!

When I was a young girl, I started going to church around six years old with my big sisters. At the time, my mother didn't attend, although she was always a believer. She grew up Catholic but switched over to Christianity later in life. My two older sisters found the church first, they later ended up bringing all of us along for church, and we all began to attend regularly.

My first church was called New Liberation Presbyterian Church, and I loved it! I grew up from a young girl into a preteen in that church before we stopped attending. I can remember being so young; I didn't understand (or listen to) the messages that Pastor Williams preached each Sunday. I also didn't know the hymnal songs we sang or what they were saying while praying. I remember as a kid being far more interested in the after-church dinners than the activities beforehand. But despite what was going on in my little head and regardless of what little I understood at the time, I always felt at home in church. Our church provided a safe haven for our hearts, and my sisters and I would come and fellowship every Sunday.

The church would do contests for the children, and the children who memorized the books of the Bible were rewarded with a brand-new Bible with their name inscribed on it. I still remember to this day the Bible presented to me. It was beautiful, crisp white, and my name was inscribed in silver in the front, and the pages in between had a silver outline. I loved that Bible; it was so beautiful. I made sure to bring my Bible with me every Sunday. I didn't really understand how much more important IN that Bible was versus what it looked like on the outside. I also didn't understand yet how much I needed God in my life, but I realized it as time went on.

You see, having God in your life, in your heart, and your corner is what can save you and keep you hanging in there. God is in full control over everything in our lives. We go through some of the things because we put ourselves in that situation and yet, and still, he is always there to give us what we need to survive and keep going.

One of my early lessons as a little girl at New Liberation was never to question God. I always knew that it was never ok to question God because whatever was going on was in his will. So, growing up with that mentality in the back of my mind, I was always more inclined to ask God to help me instead of question why. As I got older, I learned that you tend to grow through what you go through, and after my failed relationships, nothing could be more true. Each of my relationships taught me something valuable, and during them, I always felt God's presence.

Of the three major relationships I talked about earlier in the book, I can elaborate on just how God worked each situation out for me. It's truly amazing once you are out of it and able to look back and see how God's hand on your life saved you.

Beginning with my first real relationship, as I mentioned earlier, this relationship broke me down and caused me to feel so much turmoil. I felt tortured and confused because I didn't want to be in an abusive relationship, but I was too afraid to leave. So I did not know what I should do or where I should turn. I feared for my life, my safety, and that of my son's. I didn't know what he was capable of because he truly was out of his mind a lot of the time.

I remember feeling helpless, embarrassed, and sad. I wanted to be in a better situation not just for me but more so for my son, who I'd do anything in the world for and would give my life to protect. So I did the only thing that I knew, without a doubt, had the power to change my circumstances and prayed to God. Like the Smokie Norful song says, "I need you now"... My prayer was very urgent and earnest in letting God know that I needed him to step in and fix the mess I'd gotten myself into. I was afraid to leave my house, I was scared to talk to anybody about it, I was scared for my son, and I needed God to make it all go away. Well, through my prayer and my faith that he would help me, God most certainly put his hedge of protection around me and saved me from the hell on earth I was going through. I knew I needed to let go and let God!

God stepped in and made that fear go away once my tormentor was put in jail. Not just that, but the Bible says he will do "exceedingly and abundantly above all that we ask" in Ephesians 3:20. He did just that for me because by the time my son's father was released, God had blessed me with different living arrangements (somewhere much further away), a better car, and a better job so that I could begin to start my life over and provide for my son in a healthy and happy environment. I finally had peace. I knew without a doubt that God and my faith in God are what saved me. I knew that I could have easily been dead had that abusive situation continued to progress. God saved me, and I am so grateful for his grace and mercy. I could've been dead... **God handled that.**

My next relationship was smooth and not very tumultuous, but I began to get much more involved in church during this relationship. My brother in law was a pastor, and I learned a lot and applied it to my life. Of course, over time, I began to feel guilty about living with my boyfriend, aka "in sin." I wanted to be married if I was going to live with somebody, and unfortunately, our relationship was not ready for all of that. I had mentioned it to him, and although he wasn't opposed to it, he just was opposed to doing it right then and there. So again, I prayed and asked God to help me. Before I knew it, I'd finally gotten to a place where I was confident and comfortable enough to break off the relationship. I once again decided to let go and let God, and once I did, it was like a weight being lifted. I felt nothing but peace with my decision to end things. **God handled that.**

Finally, we get to my relationship with my husband of over sixteen years. This relationship was jam-packed with many prayers throughout the duration. I mean, I didn't think that things could worsen than my first relationship or that I could be hurt or brokenhearted any more than in my first one, but it happened. As you can imagine, after reading many of the things I went through, I endured a lot! I prayed and had faith that God would step in and change my husband, but he never changed. Looking back, I believe that it wasn't God's will for him to change; it was for me to learn and grow. After a while, my prayers changed, and I started praying for God to reveal if this relationship was right or not. I wanted God to tell me or better yet, show me if I should stay in the relationship. I needed God to reveal to me if this was my forever or not. There were so many things that happened, and my heart had been abused, but I was too afraid to leave. We had been together for most of my adult life. We had both grown up together and shared beautiful boys. God knew that the thing I wanted the most was for my marriage to work, but I only wanted it if it was going to be right. Please, God, show me if this is right? I needed God to show me if this was right? I wouldn't leave unless God gave me a clear sign to go.

I repeatedly asked God to restore my heart for my husband but only if it would be right for me. I didn't want to be in a situation where I was back looking stupid. I wanted God to help me stand strong through it all, but I only had the desire to do that if this man would do and be right by me. Show me who he is God; please don't let me waste any more of my life with a not right person. God knew my heart, my desires, and my cut off point. This is how I knew that God helped me out of my marriage because God knew that I would not stand for not one more infidelity. God knew, and my husband knew it too, that I was not going to even try to make it work. He could have done many things in the relationship, and I would have forgiven him, or we could have worked through it. After all, he isn't perfect, and neither am I, but there was that one thing that no matter how many years we had invested or how much I loved him or our family, that I wasn't going to accept any longer. I wasn't going to be able to restore my love and respect for this man, and I would not be able to stand strong through something that was not right. Remember how I just said we go through things to grow through things… I have never once questioned the reasoning behind my husband choosing to cheat with a friend, because that last infidelity was just the thing that would give me the answer I'd been praying for, validating for me that he indeed was NOT right. That infidelity was the door for me to get my life back, and I saw it as such almost immediately. So yes, I am so grateful because… **God handled that.**

My relationship with God is also what has contributed the most to my healing. It has healed my heart & mind. I don't know many people who could get over a failed marriage of fourteen years in less than a few weeks. I can only credit God with giving me the strength to stand tall in my decision, knowing that the unknown was most definitely worth it in the end. Sure, things may be quite difficult, and I would be traveling in rough terrain, but I was in full belief that it would be greater, later!

I didn't have any time nor desire to second guess or wallow in my loss. I also didn't have any bitterness or ill feelings towards my ex or the friend he cheated with. I wished them both healing more than anything else because I am aware that they both have deep-rooted issues plaguing them. What do I gain by holding hate in my heart for either of them? The only thing that does is stall my healing and stunt my growth! My girlfriends and some of my family members were seemingly angrier than me and couldn't understand my level of calmness and my lack of desire to "get even" or bring out pettiness. Don't get me wrong. I had a few slip-ups due to some of the outrageous things I've had to deal with while trying to get the actual divorce from my ex. Hence, I indeed had a few moments where I had a slip of the tongue or posted a few subliminal memes, but for the most part, I kept it very classy. All of this control and inner peace can be attributed to my Lord and savior.

I can honestly say that after my relationship ended, I experienced happiness from a deep place within. A happiness that I'd spent years yearning for and praying for. There is no other way to explain it or justify it, but I knew it was all because of God. Suppose you don't believe much of anything else that I have shared with you. In that case, I want you to please know and believe that God can and will help you out of a bad relationship. Still, you have to be able to recognize the out when it happens, and you have to be ready and willing to leap out in faith knowing that God is handling it one way or another, and you will indeed be greater later!

Lesson 5

Control your Insecurities & Esteem

Insecurities

As we begin to dive deeper into cause and effect related to relationships, we have to consider both insecurities and low self-esteem. Now, this is the time we have to get real with ourselves, ladies. Trust me. I get it. Nobody, and I mean **NO** body likes to admit that they have low self-esteem or have all these insecurities, but in reality, we all have experienced this at some point in time. Many have experienced both, and many people still struggle with the two. How do I know? Well, for one, I am no different than you, so of course, I struggle too. But, outside of that, another reason I know is because of the things we as women will sometimes accept. It happens a lot within a relationship; we will accept things that we know we shouldn't. It is clear because we aren't leaving that toxic relationship. Maybe it is clear because we keep attracting the same type of relationship, or perhaps we are exhibiting it in how we present ourselves. At the end of the day, you don't love yourself enough, nor will you be able to cultivate and enjoy a healthy relationship unless you learn how to manage your esteem and insecurities.

When you don't manage your insecurities and self-esteem, you may operate within the negative mindset that you have about yourself, whether you know it or not. It will not matter how many times people on the outside tell you that you're beautiful, you're smart, and you are amazing... if you can't see it within yourself. You have to learn to dig as deep as you have to go until you finally get to the core of your negative beliefs, and then you make a conscious effort to counter it and heal from it by finding ways to build it up within. That can mean different things for different people. For some, you may get back into church and start focusing on growing closer to God. In doing this, you most certainly will get a confidence boost because the closer you grow to God, the more you will experience true unconditional love & security in your life. There is no love greater than God's. See, the true reality of it is this; you will only get your insecurities and esteem in check when you stop caring about what *anyone else thinks* but **you** and **God**. God is who made you; he created you for a purpose, so you already know he thinks the world of you, now it is time for you to catch up.

Yes, I know many of us out there who pride ourselves on not giving an "F" about what anybody else thinks. We stand firm in what we believe and dismiss others' negative opinions about us without a second thought. But then that still leaves you with your own thoughts and beliefs. You may block out the outside noise of others' thoughts and opinions and not let any of that bother you, but how do you block out your own?

Why are you staying with that abusive man, sis? He constantly criticizes you. He doesn't respect you; he puts his hands on you and makes you feel like you have to walk around on eggshells. I remember these exact feelings myself. I've been there. I know how it feels when he treats you like no love ever existed. You begin to wonder, was it all a dream, did you imagine all of that love you shared before? You start wondering if you're going crazy or if there is something wrong with you. As subtle as the concern may be, there's sometimes a seed deeply planted in your mind that you're being treated like this as a result of something you did or caused.

You over there, may I ask why you are staying with that cheater? Oh, is it because he seemed genuinely sorry? Is it because he cried out real tears and swore to you, swore to God, swore on his kids, his grandmother, and put it on his life that he would never do it again? Did he threaten to kill himself because he can't stand the thought of losing you or the relationship? Is it the kids? Or maybe he agreed to give you his passcodes to his cell phone and social media accounts? Ask yourself, why are you staying with this guy? Is your answer because you love him? Are you going to tell me that you are in love with somebody who doesn't love you? Nah… I don't care about any of that stuff he's said or done to try to convince you that he's changed and he loves you too much ever to do it again because the truth of the matter is, if he loved you in the way you need and deserve to be loved, he would have never done it in the first place. Real love isn't selfish or self-serving, and although he may think and even believe he loves you, he doesn't know what real love is. Real love does indeed exist, though, but it has to start within. You see, they can't love you with that real love because they don't even know how to love themselves with that real love; otherwise, they wouldn't have disrespected themselves or the relationship for selfish gain.

Many people are out here trying to fill a void within, and they go about it the wrong way. They are walking around hurt, broken, and lost. But let me tell you something, it is not our job to fix what is broken in other people. Our only responsibility is to heal ourselves. You are staying with somebody that you can never "fix" simply because you love him or her, is just an example of you needing healing within yourself. You are not loving yourself enough if you are allowing yourself to be mistreated. You know that man or woman is lying and can't be trusted, but you are afraid of letting go. You want to believe them so badly because that feels much better than believing the truth about the hard decision you have to make. You have to decide whether you are okay with this or are you worth more.

This is where self-esteem and insecurities play a part. If you don't Love yourself with a cup that runneth over, how can you expect anyone else to? If you don't believe that you are a precious gem that must be held in the highest regard, who else will? You see, we are the ones who teach people how to treat us. I know you have heard that before, but it is true. If at the first sign of disrespect, you were poof gone, you can best believe your mission would be accomplished. He or She would learn that lesson loud and clear!

Finding out your significant other has been shady and then you checking them, or cussing them out and making them suffer for a while is NOT teaching them anything, except to be craftier. If you want them to learn, they need to know and understand they only get one chance. And guess what, if they can't comply, they will be outside looking for you with a flashlight in the daytime, wondering where you went and why they have no access to you anymore. I am not saying that people can't make mistakes and you shouldn't allow for that, because that is unrealistic. What I am saying is that inevitable "mistakes" are more like choices, and if you are choosing to hurt or disrespect another person, you deserve to be left in the dirt. Then you have officially schooled them on how not to treat a real woman. They will be able to take that experience and apply it to their life and prayerfully in their next relationship (because yes, you are gone for good), they will make wiser decisions.

One of the things I am referring to loving yourself enough refers to this matter of holding yourself in high regard. No matter how bad it hurts, no matter the costs, always choose to love yourself enough to accept nothing less than you deserve. Now, all we have to make sure of is that you understand your worth and that you believe you deserve nothing but the best. You have to know that you are more than enough for Mr./Mrs. Right. God has crafted someone who will love every little thing about you, even those weird annoyances that others haven't appreciated. If you like to sing country songs at the top of your lungs in the shower or you like to bite your man's shoulders and arms randomly, there is someone out there who will love it. They may bite your ass back, though!

No, but on a serious note, it all starts in your mind and with your beliefs. You have to believe it. Believe that God made you perfect, and there isn't anything wrong with you. Believe that you are a Queen, and you will not come up off your chariot for anyone who doesn't exhibit a true King's behaviors. He will see your value; you will not have to prove it to him. But none of that can happen until you see it for yourself.

Self Esteem
One thing about Insecurities is that they also feed into lowering your self-esteem. Now when it comes to self-esteem, comedian Katt Williams said it best. In his comedy bit titled "The Pimp Chronicles," he said something that I believe to be true, and that is that you should not be looking to others to build up your self-esteem. It is called self-esteem for a reason; you need to esteem yourself!!

Low self-esteem leaves you feeling incompetent, unlovable, and with a lack of confidence. There are so many instances and ways that low self-esteem can easily develop from your unchecked insecurities. As I mentioned above, we all have insecurities. They can come from various things such as your childhood, negative beliefs about yourself, bad relationships, abuse, rejection, or trauma. Many times there is a lot of baggage we deal with from our past. We have experienced some things that work to tear us down from the inside out. What happened to you wasn't your fault, but how you deal with it is indeed your responsibility. You can either lay down and accept defeat and darkness, or you can rise like the strong woman you and I both know you are and take your rightful place as a Queen.

I get it. Like I have shared with you before, I, too, had insecurities developed based on experiences. My first relationship made me very insecure. I always felt like I wasn't enough or like I was incapable of loving a man correctly. He had me feeling like I couldn't ever do anything right. I used to feel so bad that I would cry thinking that I was broken. He'd say things like, "I didn't know how to take care of my man right" or "I was too quiet and didn't talk enough." He would call me all the time and get mad because I didn't have much conversation for him. I hated talking on the phone. I hated it so much, but he still called me all the time wanting to talk, and he could barely carry the conversation. I can remember when he hurt my feelings so bad about not having enough conversation that I began writing down different topics to discuss while we were on the phone so I wouldn't get talked down to for not having much to say. How silly is that?? I'd have a list of things I wrote down to talk about because he wanted to talk on the phone all the time about nothing. But you know what I learned once I looked back at this time. I realized that I might have had some low self-esteem then, but I always loved myself. I loved myself enough not to change who I was, no matter the pressure. No, I didn't show him a boatload of affection, I wasn't all over him and kissing and hugging on him as if my life depended on it, because guess what? It wasn't me. I wasn't able to be that ride or die chick he wanted because I refused to help him with criminal activities. No, sir, I am not riding or dying; even in those insecure days, I had enough sense to ask where we were riding and why we have to die?!? In other words, I made sure to steer clear of anything that would put my ass in jail or worse. So yes, even back then, I am proud to see that I never totally surrendered my love for myself or my life. I didn't quite love myself enough to leave that relationship when I probably should have. This is why I always say "enough." I'd like to believe that we all love ourselves, but do we love ourselves enough?

Here are a few steps you can take to ensure that you are moving in love and light and not inundated by negative beliefs about yourself.

The first step is letting go of the past. You have got to forgive those who hurt you in the past and let that go. I don't care who it was and how bad they hurt you; forgiving them is for you, not for them. You will release yourself from bondage once you let that stuff go. You do not have to live your life with that hanging over your head. You are free to choose differently for yourself now. You also need to forgive yourself. You are human, and we all make mistakes. Show me a person out there who has never made a mistake! You have to forgive yourself for what you may have accepted or done in the past that contributed to how your life has turned out. You have to know and understand that everything you've gone through is for a reason, even if learning a valuable lesson. The only way the mistakes you made in the past are in vain are if you don't learn from them. Grow through what you go through and keep pushing forward.

Next, get to a place of acceptance. You have to become one with acceptance. Accept that you are who you are, and there is nothing wrong with who you are. Accept that you may not be able to do as much as she can or cook as well as her over there, or maybe you can't pray as flawlessly as she can (I'm talking to myself up in here), but what you can do is just fine and what you can't do you can always work on and improve. You also need to accept that you can't change the past, only the future. Accept that everything that has happened up until this point was necessary to get you to where you are today and who you will be tomorrow. Accept and know that all of who you are and who you are not is enough for the person that God has crafted for you. No one will love you correctly, like the person God has sent to love you. So take solace in acceptance because God doesn't make mistakes.

Lastly, I know you guys are probably tired of me saying this but bear with me here. You have to practice self-love. Every chance you get, love on yourself in every way possible. I don't mean this in a selfish or self-absorbed way. No, what I mean is that you have to take intentional steps towards loving yourself. Love is an action word, is it not? That's why it is not enough to say you love yourself. What are you doing to show that you love yourself? No matter how big or how small, you have to find ways to practice self-love. You can do like Mary Jane in the hit show "Being Mary Jane" and write positive affirmations about yourself on sticky notes and place them on your mirror. You can take time for yourself and slow down, relax, and get pampered. You can indulge in a cheat meal or dessert here and there. You can fill your mind with positive content and materials to help you grow. Or you can do simple things that make you feel good, like dancing, drinking tea, or drinking a glass of wine after work.

Whatever it is that makes you feel like you are giving yourself the big hug you need, do that!! Be intentional about these moments because they are important. Make sure you are walking with your head high, practice good posture. After all, a queen doesn't walk around, looking defeated. Put on pretty clothes and or accessories even if you are quarantined as many of us are at the time I am writing this book. Be sure to style your hair in a cute style that works for you, and then you show the world who you are. If you look good on the outside, it will help you feel good on the inside, so although we don't need to dress up every day all prim and pretty, it doesn't hurt to throw that in there as often as you can. You want to show love to yourself from the inside out so much so that it radiates out and shows others too.

How you feel about yourself shows itself in the decisions you make in your life and your relationships. The great news is that you always have the power to change your circumstances, good or bad. My dear, you are influencing the world around you, and you have everything inside of you that is needed to ensure you're living your best life. You have to remember who you are, Queen, and remind yourself often never to forget that you are a valuable gem. Either they will respect that and come up to your level of standards, or they will find themselves without the pleasure of your company or time. Period.

Lesson 6

Love Yourself *Enough*

Okay, okay, I know you guys have noticed this chapter's particular recurring theme several times throughout this book. That is because loving yourself enough is incredibly important and requires intention! Many times we are under the impression that we are valuing ourselves, but then we turn around and allow ourselves to be devalued in some relationships. My past relationships really helped me to see that I was allowing myself to be devalued. Anytime you are sticking with a relationship with a person who disrespects you, you are devaluing yourself. A person that talks down to you, hits you, hurts you, or belittles you is a person who obviously doesn't value you. Or perhaps they do see some value in you but guess what, it's not enough. Maybe they do actually love you but guess what, it's not enough. This is why it is so important for you to love yourself enough so that you will not accept anyone loving you in a partial or discounted way. Remember always to value yourself high and give no discounts to anybody!

Do you remember when you were a little girl and all the daydreams you had about how good life was going to be as soon as you became an adult? Do you remember playing that game with the origami paper folds where you pick a number which then leads to you picking a color and then a name, and once you get to the end, you unfold your final choice to see what your future fate held? One choice would be something like: You are going to be married, have kids, be rich and live in a mansion while another choice maybe you will be broke and live in the projects with no car. I can remember being super relieved whenever I got a good fortune, and I'd demand to do it all over again if the results were terrible. When I was a little girl, my hopes and dreams for myself were limitless. I daydreamed all the time about living the good life, having money, having a family, and being in a loving marriage. Do you remember what you used to dream your life was going to be like as a little girl? Do you remember the hopefulness that you had? Can you recall how happy inside you felt thinking about it? Now, what if you had a chance to go back to one of those moments and speak to your younger self. Let's transport ourselves back and walk up to our younger selves. I want you to imagine looking yourself into your own eyes and looking into all of the hopefulness, anticipation, and eagerness that lies within the heart and mind of your younger self. Let's say that she excitedly has run up to you and given you a big hug; she is in awe of seeing herself as an adult and is relishing in how beautiful you are. She's very proud to see her future self and wants to know if her origami life came true?? If you had to tell her at that moment what her future mate was like, would you be proud or ashamed? If you were to tell your younger self that you were taking care of yourself and loving yourself enough, would you be telling yourself the truth?

I know. It is not an easy process when you begin to be honest with yourself. Sometimes with being honest, you will see that a major or drastic change needs to happen. If learning to finally love yourself fully and enough calls for you to learn that you deserve more and will not accept anything less, then that also may mean ending your current relationship if it isn't healthy. I want you to love yourself in a way that you would be happy and proud to go back and tell that little girl.

The good news is that things get better. Everything around you gets better when you start to love yourself enough to value yourself high up to the sky!! Yes! I said high up to the sky because you absolutely need to think the highest of yourself so that you immediately recognize when someone else is trying to devalue you in any way. Once you get to that level, life opens up even more for you. The probability of you going back to an abusive ex decreases significantly when you reach that level. The probability of you entering into a relationship with another timewaster will lessen. You see, because now you are walking around like the prize you are, and you are not allowing just anybody to have the privilege of accessing you or your love. You begin to finally realize that you really have everything you need within. You know that you were fearfully and wonderfully made. You do not need anyone else to validate you in any way.

Bittersweet Lessons

Part 3

The Escape Route

Bittersweet Lessons

The Escape Route

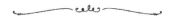

Through my experiences in loving and leaving, I learned a lot. They say hindsight is 20/20, and BABBYYYY they are right. Some of the things that I learned I wished someone had given me a heads up about so that I could have saved myself some time and heartache. So since I didn't have that someone, I am going to be that someone. So with that sentiment in mind, I came up with "The Escape Route," which is a guideline around eight common stages of a breakup. I call it the escape route because once you get through these stages, you are finally free of the bondage of your turbulent relationship. You are free in your heart, mind, body, and soul and can move forward. If you take these steps, you will make it out and come out better and stronger! Whether you see it or know it or not, once you make it out of the escape route… you sis, have GROWN! Here are the eight stages:

Stage 1. Enlightenment

In this stage, you are beginning to really open your eyes to what is really going on. You are beginning to understand that you have been dealing with a bunch of BS, possibly dealing with lots of lies, and have been probably lying to yourself about the reality of what's going on. This stage is when you are beginning to see that your mate is not right for you, doesn't meet your standards, and you aren't very happy.

In this stage, you may be feeling bamboozled, confused, and disappointed. I need you to use this time to gather up all your information. This is where you are finally faced with the facts. What I mean by that is I want you to really take the time to sit and think about what is going on without making excuses or trying to justify his (or her) actions. Separate the facts from your feelings. Your intuition is likely what got you here to this point, so I need you to use this time to substantiate what is actually going on. You need to get the proof and/or the confirmation that what you know deep down in your gut is true.

Stage 2. The Epiphany

The next stage is what I like to call the "Epiphany Moment." You should be comparing what you deserve to what you have been experiencing, and once it isn't adding up to you, this is when it's like you suddenly wake up and smell the coffee. You finally see through all of the smoke screens, the lies, fraud, and deceit and are clear as ever on the reality of the situation at hand. In this stage, you are feeling a sort of a-ha moment where things become perfectly clear. You know, without a doubt, what is going on, and you are ready to accept it.

In this stage, you should clear your mind of the "what ifs" and stop yourself from trying to justify for that other person. Rid yourself of the fear and focus instead on faith. Now is the time to trust your gut!

Stage 3. Acceptance

The acceptance stage is when you are ready to accept that the relationship is over and no longer serves you or your needs.

This stage allows you to come to terms with acceptance that this actually is the end. You are clear and accepting that the person you have been with this whole time is not the person you need to be with. You understand that your happiness is at stake, and you are the only person who can make the changes. It is not always your fault for the things you have been through, but it is always your responsibility to accept and make the necessary changes when possible.

Stage 4. The Decision

In the decision phase, you have accepted that the relationship isn't going to work, and now you are making the decision to actually leave. After realizing the truth and taking in what's going on and then accepting that things must change, you have to make the decision to stay or to leave.

You have no doubt about what you need to do, and now is the time to step out on faith and move forward with that decision. You are clear on the task at hand, knowing that this is for the best. Yes, it may hurt, and you may have some fear or reservations on the finality of ending things but, you know deep down inside that this is the right thing to do and so you decide once and for all to just do it.

Stage 5. The Plan

The planning stage is when you put your plan in place to make your move. This could mean you figuring out your future living situation, your financial needs, and/or just planning out how you will break the news to everyone impacted.

Take this time to really think everything through from A to Z. Put a plan in place that allows for reasonable and proper timing of getting things done. But don't take too long, because the longer you take, you run the risk of falling back into the cycle of that bad relationship. If you live with your partner, you will have to decide if you are going to move out, move them out, or put on a 30-day notice. If you share children together, you will need to start thinking about how you both will co-parent. Put a plan in place that will ensure that you and your children will have what you need. You are now ready to take action!

Stage 6. Action

The Action phase is when you finally take action, and you go! You have now taken the necessary steps to get out of the relationship in the physical form, and you are now moving onward and upward.

You have now officially and/or physically moved on from this situation. Whether that means you have kicked them to the curb, or you've packed up all of your items and moved out, or if this simply means you have finally broken the news to that other person. This is it! This is when you take back your life and gain your freedom. You are feeling a great sense of relief, and you should be very proud of yourself. Embrace this moment and relish in the fact that you were brave and strong enough to move in your best interest! You love yourself enough to choose you and your happiness over your fears, your insecurities, and your convenience or comfort. You should be proud because you have officially removed a person out of your life that simply does not deserve you.

Stage 7. Commitment

In the commitment phase, you are now moving along in your new reality. You are committing to yourself to keep looking forward and not back. You should walk boldly into your future without any regrets for doing what was best.

You may feel tinges of uncertainty or even regret in some moments, but they will be fleeting as long as you stand firm in the commitment you made to yourself. This is your life, and you have taken steps to improve it. But it will only improve if you stay committed to your decision. You know it was the right decision, so I need you to listen to your head and not your heart and keep pushing forward. This feeling shall pass, and you will come out on the other side, feeling absolutely fabulous!!

Stage 8. Peace

Once you have taken all of the previous steps, you will finally reach the final step in the process in which you attain peace. The peace you feel will come from deep within and will permeate your heart and soul. The peace you feel will be rewarding and well worth the heartache up until this point.

For this stage, I like to think of it as you are reaching that final level and finally attaining that glow! (FYI: my favorite movie just so happens to be *The Last Dragon*) You are going to feel so much peace, relief, and gratefulness inside that you will literally feel like you are glowing from the inside out. You will feel so much love inside for yourself and so much appreciation and pride in making the right decision even though it was the hard decision. You will realize that you have survived another storm, crossed another bridge, and have indeed come out stronger on the other side. There were some lessons that you have learned, and you are thankful for that. You have grown, and you are better.

Letting Go

Once you have ended your relationship and gone through the phases of the escape route, I wish that I could say that you are free & clear from this point on, but the reality is that you still have more work to do. One of the things you must commit to is really letting go. This means you have got to really let go of the past, let go of the pain, the shame, the embarrassment, and any bitterness. You have to figure out a way to forgive your ex and then also forgive yourself. This is a must if you truly want to thrive moving forward. Everything is attached to a choice, and you've chosen to improve your world. But also remember, whether you believe it or not, healing is also a choice that you make. Forgiveness is a choice that you make. Letting go is also a choice that you now have to make.

Final Chapter

The Glow

"Level Up" - Ciara

Bittersweet Lessons

The one thing that almost always happens after a breakup is a renewed sense of self. We usually start getting our workout regimen back on, our hair & nails done regularly, and start dressing extra cute, all while still healing. It happens every time, am I right? It's like we are just now remembering to go hard for ourselves. Love on ourselves a little more. You may have always worked out or always kept your hair/nails done throughout the relationship. I guarantee that you more than likely went a little harder or put a little extra pizazz into yourself once you finally were free of a bad relationship. Now is the time to actively seek out your happiness! Whether it's spending more time with your friends, going to the spa, or enjoying your own company, you must do what makes you happy. You deserve it, so relish in it.

Now is the time sis, now is the time to shine from the inside out. I mean, I promise you that I felt like I was glowing after I reached this point. I felt like life had just begun and that the best was yet to come. My marriage ended months before my 40th birthday. Never had I imagined that I'd be single, nor a single mom at 40! I didn't see that coming at all but trust me when I tell you that turning 40 was like a catalyst to me turning the corner and finally choosing to love myself... enough. I was finally genuinely happy. I wasn't concerned about the past failures any longer because the future was (and is) much too bright.

This special breaking out point I like to call leveling up in happiness. At this time, you should begin to learn more about yourself and free yourself from all of the things holding you back from being truly happy. Forgive yourself for what you took yourself through or things you feel like you caused or allowed to happen. Take all the hurt, shame, and disappointments of the past and throw it all behind you, never to look back.

Congratulations!!! You are now at the level up stage.

The level up stage is when you begin to walk in your destiny. God created each of us for a reason, and we all have gifts and talents. For me, in my level-up stage, I began to gravitate towards anything uplifting and positive. I looked for podcasts, books, and social media pages tailored for growth. I wanted to get better in every area of my life and began to level up in my spiritual walk, in my finances, and my health. I made sure to feed my mind content and things that would further my growth. After a while, many of my friends and loved ones began to see a change in me; it was like a shift happened. I felt myself morphing into a better me. A new and improved version of myself was developing… after while Nichole Cooper was let go of and Nikki Nichole was unearthed. Once you have let go of the toxic situations in your life, you will see a shift in how much love & light get ushered in. You will shy away from any negativity and gravitate towards growth and positivity!

Nikki Nichole is so much better than she used to be. Can I just brag on Nikki Nichole for a second because I am so very proud of her! I just need to say that I am not mentioning any of this to brag arrogantly. I am not better than you. I am mentioning it because I had no idea what I was capable of accomplishing until I got to this place. I am proud of myself because things most definitely could have turned out differently, and far worse. I tell you because if "I" can level up and survive my previous toxic situations, then girlfriend, so can you!!

Sometimes we as women are our toughest critics and do not spend enough time being happy with or for ourselves, which is a sign you aren't loving yourself enough. I love me some Nikki Nichole because she has been through a lot, and is still standing, growing, and glowing. She prays daily. She makes an intentional effort daily to be positive and uplifting to other women. She also has a passion for helping other women grow, glow, and succeed. In this phase of her life, she successfully was able to get her finances in order to pay all of the bills of a household that once struggled even when it had two incomes and paychecks. Thank you, Lord! She also started a women's empowerment group on Facebook titled: Sis, Love yourself, where we cultivate a sisterhood that builds and uplifts one another. She then stepped out and became an entrepreneur starting a successful bartending training and mixology party company. She wrote a book and became a published author and speaker. She now has additional businesses & ideas in the works. Oh, and last but not least, she found love again… the healthy kind.

She has loved and lost but cherishes every lesson learned. She is a woman on a mission to continuously grow and evolve for the better. People from the past barely recognize her, and some may wonder, who does she think she is? To that I say, She is Nikki Nichole… and she…. is… the…. master. (Okay, okay, look I already warned you all that "The Last Dragon" was my favorite movie, so I had to do it, ha-ha) I am most proud of her because she has mastered the art of living, learning, and loving herself enough!

The End.

Before you go....

Now I am not here telling any of you to leave your relationships; the only thing I'd like for you to do is be honest and do some self-reflecting. I wanted to leave you with a tool that you can use to help you figure out if you should or should not leave your current relationship. That is a personal decision and not one that I, nor any of your friends or family can make for you. This is a decision that comes from digging deep, self-reflection, and prayer. If you are honest with yourself and dedicated to loving yourself, enough. This tool should help you in figuring it out because the answer is within.

How do you know if you should leave your relationship? Ask yourself these questions.

∂   Does your partner make you feel good, proud of yourself, and happy inside? Or does your partner make you feel bad about yourself, insecure, ashamed, or sad within the relationship?

∂   Does he/she make you feel like they are your biggest fan, and like you can accomplish your dreams, or do they make you question if they really support you or if they believe in you, value you or are even proud of you?

∂   Do you trust this person? Do you feel like your heart is safe with them? Or do you have that gut feeling? Is your intuition screaming to you that your partner is not always honest with you? Have you caught your partner in lies or deceit?

∂ Does your partner hold you in high regard and respect you and your opinion? Or does your partner disrespect you in any way?

Lastly, the Golden Question. I want you to really dig deep and answer honestly this one last question:

∂ Given everything you now know about this person, and everything you have experienced due to this relationship. If you had the chance to go back and do it *all* over again with the knowledge you have today, would you repeat this relationship given these results? Would you advise that little girl of you to stay in this type of relationship or seek better?

About the Author

Nikki Nichole is a mom of three sons, an entrepreneur, author, and women's empowerment specialist coach. She grew up in San Francisco, CA as the youngest of four girls to a single mother. Growing up in a poverty-stricken area she flourished as best she could but always struggled with inner feelings of not being good enough.

Through personal development, spiritual growth, a mindset change, and a shift in trajectory she evolved into a forward-looking, bold & confident woman inciting her inner healing transition. This shift opened the door for genuine self-love & true happiness to finally enter in. It sparked a flame inside leading Nikki towards a purpose driven path.

As a result, Nikki has developed into an author, and women's empowerment coach. She's the creator of a women's empowerment movement and FB group called "Sis, Love Yourself" which is geared towards women supporting each other & loving themselves *enough* to leave behind anything that doesn't serve them.

Nikki also started one of her first businesses "Baytenders" which is a bartending school & mixology party service along with a branding business and currently she hosts a weekly women's virtual book club centered around women's growth & development. To learn more about Nikki Nichole, and what she has in the works please visit: www.sheisnikkinichole.com

Made in the USA
Coppell, TX
29 January 2023